PATIENT CONFIDENTIALITY

Edito
John
Read
Notti
The N

£25.33
T/

A021635

W 32

© EMIS Professional Publishing and the Authors 2002

Published by
EMIS Professional Publishing Ltd
31–33 Stonehills House
Welwyn Garden City
Hertfordshire
AL8 6PU

ISBN 1 85811 296 6

Typeset by Jane Conway

Cover design by Jane Conway
Cover photography by Jon Adams

Printed in Great Britain by Antony Rowe

List of Contributors

John Tingle, Reader in Health Law, Director of the Centre for Health Law, Department of Academic Legal Studies, Nottingham Law School, The Nottingham Trent University

Kay Wheat, Senior Lecturer in Law, Department of Academic Legal Studies, Nottingham Law School, The Nottingham Trent University

Dr. David Bainbridge, Reader in Law, Aston Business School, Aston University, Birmingham

Dr. Alan O'Rourke, Lecturer, Insitute of General Practice and Primary Care, Sheffield University

Sandy Anthony, Writer and Editor, The Medical Protection Society, Risk Consulting

Sean Riddell (Deputy Managing Director EMIS) and Chris Spencer (Solicitor and Product Development Director, EMIS Legal)

Rob McSherry, Principal Lecturer Practice Development, Postgraduate Institute, School of Health and Social Care, University of Teeside

Paddy Pearce, Clinical Governance Manager, Friarage Hospital, Northallerton, South Tees Hospital NHS Trust

Dr Richard Griffin, Consultant, Chichester NHS Trust

Mary Hawking, Senior Partner (EMIS Practice), Kingsbury Court Surgery, Dunstable, Beds.

Dedicated to

Rachel, Rebecca, Gillian
and to our dearly departed Marmaduke

CONTENTS

TABLE OF CASES

TABLE OF STATUTES AND MATERIALS

Regulations

PREFACE

The aim of this book is to provide a number of informed perspectives on the issue of confidentiality of health care records. The chapters are designed to highlight the dilemmas faced by GP's, patients and other health care professionals as they try to comply with the law and Government policy in the area on health care records.

The book contains an interesting collection of chapters written by a wide group of professionals, academics, lawyers and health care professionals and managers. The view is taken that in order to obtain the complete picture of issues a holistic approach to the legal issues must be taken. Legal issues are explored along with other practical issues and Government policy directives and initiatives.

This is a dynamic and changing field and this book provides the reader with a essential further reading and web sources to keep up-to-date.

I would like to thank Andrew Griffin of EMIS Professional Publishing for his enthusiasm and support during the writing of the text and my colleague Kay Wheat for her reviews of sections of the book and indeed her own chapter.

John Tingle
Nottingham
July 2002

INTRODUCTION
A QUESTION OF CONFIDENCE

John Tingle, Reader in Health Law, Nottingham Law School, The Nottingham Trent University

The Importance of Health Records

There is a saying amongst health lawyers and those concerned with risk management in the NHS, 'that in court, you are only as good as your records'. 'No records, no defence' is another well known saying, equally succinct and meaningful. Clearly health records are important as they provide a real-time record of what went on between patient and health carer and they can, in practical terms, determine whether or not a clinical negligence action is won or lost.

Health records are also an important mechanism of communication in health care. Many commentators in clinical risk management and health litigation would argue that one of the main causes of complaints and litigation is failures in communication. Records may have been lost or not passed on to relevant colleagues. The patient may have been told, or not told something when they should have been. Relatives may not have been informed about a key matter when a patient relative is discharged into their care.

Health care records are also an important mechanism of health care management and accountability with the information contained in health records being used for a variety of purposes. Chapters in this book will explore the possible uses. Records make the NHS move, and without them everything would grind to a halt.

A Balancing of Competing Interests?

Information is control and without the information contained on health records our NHS system could not be properly managed.

All the above said, it is clear that health care information needs to be shared through the system. But health records are not ordinary records. They are documents or data which contain some very personal information about a person's medical condition. The information by its very nature is confidential and the health carers who take down the information are under professional and legal duties not to reveal that information.

A balance or a trade off has therefore to be achieved in managing the NHS, and respecting the confidences of its patients.

This book has been designed to give information to help the reader assess whether this balance has been correctly achieved, where the line has been drawn and the problems and good practices in the area.

Confidentiality Is Not Just About Law

Confidentiality and health care records is a developing and dynamic topic and involves a variety of areas of knowledge and expertise. It must not be seen solely a legal topic but also as a topic that involves other disciplines such as medicine, nursing, health care management, health care ethics, health care politics and clinical risk management. In order to obtain the full picture a variety of perspectives must be considered, and this is the approach followed in the book.

Hard and Soft Law

It will be seen that there is an established body of law on the topic which is developing. There are Statutes and cases which govern the area, this can be termed the, 'hard law'. However in researching the area for this book it has become very apparent that there is also a wealth of so called, 'soft law': Government policy documents, circulars, advisory documents etc.. This book has tried to concentrate on the hard law side, but for completeness we have included a reasonable amount of 'soft law' in order to give the full picture.

Confidentiality, Politics and the Patient

It has already been acknowledged above that the law cannot be looked at in isolation from what is happening with Government policy on health records and confidentiality. The NHS Plan, Clinical Governance, Patient Empowerment are all Government policy initiatives which are focussed on changing the culture of the NHS towards the patient.[1] To summarise Government policy in health: it is unquestionably, that the patient is the most important person in the care equation and that the NHS should revolve around patient interests and not those of the health carers within the NHS. The patient is to be king in the new NHS.These policy views can be seen to inform current Government policies and practices in health care record keeping and confidentiality and they therefore maintain important implications for all health care professionals and managers in the NHS.

The Government pace of reform in the area is fast and there always appears to be development, for example, the first meeting of the new Health Records and Data Protection Review Group[2] set up to advise the Government on helping people to gain access to their health records, took place on Friday 24th May 2002. The group, whose members represent patient groups, health and social care professionals and regulatory bodies will be advising the Government on:

- charges levied by Doctors, under the Data Protection Act, for providing individuals with copies of their health records;

- whether and when Doctors need to screen a patient's health records before they can see them;

- how information in a patient's medical record about their family and family history should be handled in respect of the Data Protection Act 1998; and

---

1. See further, Tingle, J.H. Chapter 5, The Policy Dimension: The Legal Environment of the New NHS,in *Nursing Law and Ethics*, Edited by J.H.Tingle and A. Cribb, 2nd Edition, 2002, Blackwell Publishing, Oxford.
2. Department of Health Press Release, 2002/0244, Monday 27th May 2002, First Meeting of New Health Records and Data Protection Review Group.

- whether conditions need to be prescribed to govern the use of the new NHS number, which is a unique number allocated to individuals.

Welcoming the establishment of the new Health Records and Data Protection Review Group, Health Minister Hazel Blears said[3]

"It is important that individuals have access to their health records so that they are better informed about their own treatment and care and can make decisions based on that information. We must work closely with all key interests to improve the procedures for providing individual's with access to their health records. The Health Records and Data Protection Review Group will play an important role in this work."

The political policy perspective is very important and there is clearly a lot happening though it seems an almost impossible task to keep up-to-date with everything that is going on in the area.

The Ethics of Health Records and Confidentiality

To add to the perspectives considered above there is also an important health care ethical perspective to health records and confidentiality and a number of ethical issues are involved such as Autonomy and Utilitarianism. As Stauch, Wheat and Tingle[4] state:

"It is not only of academic interest to look at the ethical justifications for the obligation of confidence, it is also important to keep them in mind when examining the circumstances in which the obligation can be lawfully breached, and to consider whether the breaches in question can also be justified on ethical grounds...the doctrine of utilitarianism assesses the ethics of a course of action on the basis that it will result in the best consequences overall. In the context of confidentiality, therefore, the obligation is justified by the utility of doctors keeping medical information secret. The argument is that if there is no assurance of secrecy, then patients would be reluctant to seek medical advice or treatment, or would be less than frank when doing so. This would, it is argued, have an adverse effect on the health of society..."

---

3.   Ibid.
4.   Stauch, M., Wheat, K; with Tingle,J.H., *Sourcebook on Medical Law*, 1998, Cavendish Publishing Ltd, London.

The utilitarian view is particularly appropriate to confidentiality as it will readily admit that the duty is not absolute and can be breached in certain circumstances. It would be argued that the breach is justified when the utility of disclosure outweighs the utility produced by keeping the confidences."

This paragraph sums up the issues at the heart of the confidentiality debate, some of which are explored in chapters in this book. The debates and developments in the area will be continuous and on-going and this book will provide the reader with the information and sources of further information to keep up with developments.

PART I
THE LAW

CHAPTER 1
MEDICAL CONFIDENTIALITY AND THE LAW

Kay Wheat
Senior Lecturer in Law,
The Nottingham Trent University

Introduction

It might be thought that the law relating to confidentiality is based upon the right to privacy, but there is no right to privacy that is grounded in English law. However, since the passing of the Human Rights Act of 1998, which came into force in October 2000, it has been possible to rely directly upon the European Convention on Human Rights in our domestic courts, and Article 8 of the Convention protects the right to 'a private life'. The extent to which, if at all, this makes a difference to the legal position on confidentiality, will be dealt with further below.

This chapter looks mainly at English common law – judge-made law, not law that emanates from legislation passed by Parliament. However, below there is a brief examination of statutory obligations which relate to confidential information. There is some debate as to the precise nature of the legal basis of the English common law that protects confidences. It has been said to be one or more, or a mixture, of the law based upon contract, trusts and property law. However, this is of academic interest only, as it is well established that, in the appropriate circumstances, the law protects confidences. Furthermore, as far as the practice of medicine is concerned, it is uncontroversial that the doctor/patient relationship gives rise to an obligation of confidence. Similarly, although so much of the literature focuses on doctors, medical information acquired by other health care workers is subject to the same protection. There can be circumstances in which there is, nevertheless, some doubt about whether the nature of the information is such that it should be protected. For example, it might not be medical information as such. The case of *R v Wilson* [1996] 3 WLR 125 is illustrative of this point. In that case, a husband was charged with causing his wife actual bodily harm in consequence of him having given her a homemade 'tattoo' on her buttock, using a hot knife. She had specifically asked him to do this and, throughout, made no complaint that she had not been fully compliant. However, case law is such, that for 'policy' reasons (and some would argue, for unacceptably paternalistic reasons), it is not possible to consent to actual bodily harm (outside of legitimate contexts such as *bona fide* surgical operations). In the event, the Court of Appeal overturned the man's conviction for a number of reasons, one of which being that there was little real difference between this and the creation of a tattoo by a professional tattooist. The interest, for our purposes, is in the way in which the matter came to the knowledge of the police in the first place. The woman's GP reported it, having become aware of it during the course of a medical examination. It is not known whether any action for breach of confidence was taken against him (either via the ordinary civil courts or via a complaint of professional misconduct to the General Medical Council), but although it was not medical information, there is little doubt that it would attract the protection of the law, both by its nature and the circumstances in which it was acquired. Confidences can, of course, under certain circumstances, be disclosed, but, as we shall see below, it is highly unlikely that disclosure in these sorts of circumstances could be justified. It has also been suggested that the *inadvertent* acquisition of information which clearly has the necessary quality of confidence about it, binds the recipient (see *Attorney-General* v *Guardian Newspapers (No 2)* [1990] AC 109), so the protection is not restricted to medical consultations as such.

Difficulties can arise in connection with the circumstances in which the obligation to protect confidences can be breached. One way of describing the basis upon which the law on confidentiality rests, is to emphasise that it is regarded as being in the public interest that, in certain circumstances, confidences are kept. This is nowhere more clear than in the context of medical confidences. If people did not believe that the information given to health care workers would be protected, they would be less likely to seek treatment and less likely to be frank as to the nature of their symptoms, or, for example, relevant aspects of their lifestyle. In consequence, diagnosis would be likely to be less accurate; treatment would be likely to be less effective, and there could even be reluctance to seek help of any kind. There are, therefore, clear public health benefits in protecting the obligation of confidence. It is not, however, an absolute obligation, and can be breached, but, if it is to be breached, either the patient must have consented to this, or there must be a stronger countervailing public interest in breaching the obligation.

Mention should be made of the General Medical Council guidance[1] on confidentiality. A court will consider carefully any guidelines given by professional bodies, but it must be remembered that these are not synonymous with the law. However, in this chapter, reference will be made to the guidance where appropriate.

Disclosing confidences with the consent of the patient

The patient can consent to the information being disclosed. However, problems can arise if the patient is not competent to consent i.e. is either a child or an adult lacking in capacity. As far as children are concerned, under section 8 of the Family Law Reform Act 1969 children who have attained the age of 16 can give a valid consent to treatment. However, the Court of Appeal has held that this does not oust the jurisdiction of the courts, and that the consent – or refusal – of the child under section 8 can be overridden by the court exercising its inherent jurisdiction in respect of the protection of children (see *Re W (A Minor)(Medical Treatment)* [1992] 4 All E.R. 627). Nevertheless, subject to this proviso, it is clear that the child is entitled to respect for medical confidences from the age of 16. The well-known case of *Gillick v West Norfolk and Wisbech Area Health Authority* [1986] 1 AC 112 considered the position of children under the age of 16. This case was about the provision of contraceptive advice to the under-16s, and the NHS guidance which instructed doctors, that, exceptionally, they could give such advice in confidence, i.e. without reference to the child's parents. By a majority, the House of Lords held that the policy was lawful as long as the child was *"Gillick* competent". In other words, as long as the child has sufficient understanding to be deemed to have the capacity to consent, there is no magic in the age of 16. This decision was considered by the Court of Appeal in *Re W* (see above) and a somewhat restrictive interpretation placed upon it, (which, it must be said, is not at all within the spirit of the majority decisions in *Gillick*). The court held that the consent of a child

---

1.   General Medical Council, *Confidentiality: Protecting and Providing Information*, 2000, GMC, London.

protected the doctor, but if the child refused treatment then the doctor could seek the consent of the parent(s).

How does *Gillick* and this subsequent case affect confidentiality? On a liberal view of *Gillick*, if the child has capacity, then the child has a right to the protection of confidentiality. It is accepted that this might sometimes be difficult to handle in practice. If one supposes that a doctor prescribes the contraceptive pill confidentiality to, say, a 15 year old, if that child subsequently needed treatment in which she involved her parents, it might become known to them that she was taking the contraceptive pill (for example, there might be a contraindication). Nevertheless, this is a problem of management, and could, in any event, have been anticipated by the doctor when prescribing, by warning the child of this possibility.

On a *Re W* interpretation of *Gillick*, however, it is possible to argue that the doctor is protected if he does not disclose, but also protected if he does. However, it is possible to argue that, if the doctor is treating the child who has consented, then any form of disclosure would be redundant, as it could be no part of the treatment efficacy to breach confidence. Again, in practical terms, this might mean that parents are informed, or discover through other means, what is going on. Realistically, if the parents are actively involved in their child's life, there might be occasions when they will discover what has previously been confidential between child and doctor, via another medical context. On any interpretation, even if the child is regarded as being incompetent up to the age of 16, and, depending upon the circumstances, possibly still incompetent at the age of 17, then whatever decisions are made, and that includes respecting or not respecting confidences, then such decisions must be made in the best interests of the child.

The adult who lacks medical decision-making capacity must also be treated in his or her best interests. Although there are differences in law between incompetent adults and children (legislation and the common law protecting children are wide enough to cover medical treatment, whereas the courts have floundered to find a satisfactory legal basis for decision-making on behalf of incompetent adults – see *Re F (Mental Patient: Sterilisation)* [1990] 2 AC 1, and *A v A Health Authority & others etc.* QBD Administrative Court/FAM 24/01/2002), nevertheless the "best interests" test applies. The health carers should, therefore, be protected if disclosure is made which is necessary in the best interests of the person concerned.

If the patient is competent, then normally there would be nothing controversial about them consenting to disclosure, as long as the purpose of the disclosure is made clear to them and they agree without duress. It might be argued that there can be an implied consent to disclosure, for example, to other health care professionals involved in the treatment of the patient.

Disclosing confidences in the public interest

Regardless of consent, the disclosure might be justifiable in the public interest. There is no definitive list of public interest justifications, but what follows are examples based upon case law.

The Freedom of the Press

There is a public interest in the freedom of the press. The case of *X* v *Y* [1988] 2 All E.R. 648 concerned a health authority's employment of two doctors who were being treated for AIDS. A newspaper was given the names by someone inside the health authority, and an injunction was sought by the authority, to restrain the publication of the doctors' names. The injunction was granted. The newspapers' argument had rested upon the fact that the publication would open up a necessary debate (an essential element of the public interest in the freedom of the press) on the risk associated with doctors who have AIDS or are HIV positive. The court found that this debate was going on anyway, and the public interest in protecting AIDS patients far outweighed the 'minimal' contribution to the debate that the publication would make.

The Prevention of Crime

Clearly, there is a public interest in the prevention of crime, and this was considered in the *X* v *Y* case. The argument had been, on behalf of the health authority, that there should be the disclosure by the newspaper of the person within the health authority who had given the names of the doctors to the press, because a crime had been committed contrary to the Public Bodies Corrupt Practices Act 1889 and the Prevention of Corruption Act 1906. This argument, however, was unsuccessful. It was held that there was no duty to *prosecute* crime. However, there have been a number of cases which have examined disclosure in the case of serious crime prevention, notably the case of *W* v *Egdell* [1990] 1 All E.R. 835. This concerned a mental health patient who was detained in a secure hospital pursuant to an order of the criminal court, following his conviction for a number of killings and other crimes of violence. Such patients are presently detained until such time as they are no longer a danger to others. The patient here had made an application to a mental health review tribunal with a view to being transferred to a less secure unit, and to, eventual release. The patient instructed a solicitor who, in turn, instructed a psychiatrist, Dr Egdell, to examine him and prepare a report for the tribunal. However, upon examination Dr Egdell formed the view that the patient was still dangerous, having what was described as a "long standing and abnormal interest in dangerous explosives dating from before his period of acute illness", and stated so in his report. Not surprisingly, in the absence of positive psychiatric evidence, his application was withdrawn, but the patient's case was due to come before a tribunal under the automatic review process, and Dr Egdell sent a copy of the report to the medical director of the hospital and a copy to the Home Office. An action for breach of confidence ensued. The patient was unsuccessful, and the matter went to the Court of Appeal, where disclosure to prevent serious crime was considered. The emphasis was upon the dangerousness, or potential dangerousness of this particular patient. Bingham LJ said:

> "Where a man has committed multiple killings under the disability of serious mental illness, decisions which may lead .... to his release ... should not be made unless a responsible authority is properly able to make an informed judgment that the risk of repetition is so small as to be acceptable."

This justified the release of the report. Elsewhere in the case it was stated that the risk must be "real, immediate and serious". This is also reflected in the GMC guidance[2], which states:

> "Disclosures may be necessary in the public interest where a failure to disclose information may expose the patient or others to risk of death or serious harm" (para 36).

It is arguable that the prevention of small scale, non-serious crime would not outweigh the public interest in the protection of confidences, nor would the prosecution of past crimes unless they were of considerable significance. Similarly, the reference here has been to criminal wrongs and it is unlikely that the commission of

---

2.   See footnote 1 above.

civil wrongs only (past or future) would provide a sufficiently weighty countervailing interest.

To Protect Third Parties

Disclosure can be made to protect third parties when there is no particular risk of a crime being committed. This was the case in *Re C (A Minor) (Evidence: Confidential Information)* (1991) 7 BMLR 138, which was an adoption case, in which evidence was admitted by the judge in the form of a medical report by the GP on the child's mother. This gave details of her medical condition as to how it related to her ability to look after the child. The mother appealed to the Court of Appeal, where it was actually doubted whether there had been a breach of medical confidentiality, but even if there had been it was found to be justified in the "very serious matter" of the adoption of a child. Presumably the doubt about whether there had been a breach was based on the fact that the GP was also the doctor of the proposed adoptive child. This is arguably wrong. The better way of viewing the matter is to say that there was an obligation of confidence owed to both patients, but it had to be breached in respect of the mother to protect the future of the child who had a stronger countervailing interest in disclosure of the report.

The protection of children was examined in the case of *D* v *National Society for the Prevention of Cruelty to Children* [1977] 1 All E.R. 589, where the identity of someone who had made what turned out to be an ill-founded allegation of child abuse, was not revealed on the basis that it was in the interests of the public functioning of a body such as the NSPCC, whose purpose was to protect children against ill-treatment, to keep the identity of complainants confidential. An analogy was drawn between this and the guaranteed anonymity of police informers.

Other disclosures

There is a legitimate public interest in the proper administration of justice. In court proceedings, certain documents can be ordered to be produced, witnesses can be subpoenaed and so on. If an objection is made that the disclosure or the giving of evidence raises issues of breaching confidentiality, then this should be pointed out to the judge who will then have to make a decision on disclosure. Otherwise, there is no immunity given to doctors, or other health care workers, from the normal court processes (see *Hunter* v *Mann* [1974] 1 QB 767).

Although it does not raise discrete legal issues, the whole area of HIV and AIDS raises strong emotions, such so that the GMC gives specific guidance on serious communicable diseases.[3] This is hardly surprising as these conditions attract significant, serious stigma, and also adversely affect important issues such as insurance, job security and pensions. The guidance specifically states that, both in respect of other health care workers and third parties such as a known sexual contact, the patient should be advised to disclose his or her condition. However, in the absence of an agreement to do this by the patient, the advice, which is in accordance with the law, stresses that disclosure cannot be made unless there is risk of death or serious harm, and the patient should be told about the decision to disclose and the health care worker should be able to justify the decision.

Dual responsibilities and disclosure

Just as in the situation of medical research, different considerations can arise when the doctor or other health care worker is effectively wearing two hats. This would be the case where, for example, an occupational physician or nurse, or a police or prison doctor is in receipt of information relating to the health of someone where there is no strict doctor/patient relationship. In the employment context, for example, there may be a system of routine testing because of the nature of the employment e.g. exposure to lead, and the occupational health worker will be privy to the results of such testing. Whilst there may be a statutory obligation on the employer to carry out such surveillance, e.g. under the Control of Substances Hazardous to Health (COSHH) Regulations 1988, the co-operation with such testing and disclosure of results would normally be part of the contract of employment. The situation is not so clear in cases where there is a system of health surveillance (either before or during employment), which is not based upon statutory regulation. It is important, whatever the context, for the parameters of any consultations, examinations and use of any information ascertained, to be set and understood *before* any testing or consultation takes place. The GMC[4] gives guidance to this effect in para. 34).

---

3.   General Medical Council, Serious Communicable Diseases, 1998, GMC, London www.gmc-uk.org/standards.
4.   See footnote 1 above.

The extent of the disclosure

It is important to stress that, just because some form of disclosure can be lawfully justified, this does not mean that the information can be revealed to all and sundry. In *Re C* (above), it was stressed by the court that the disclosure had been very limited in that the report on the mother had only been made available to the judge who had decided the application, which, in any event, had been a closed hearing and not in open court. In the case of *W* v *Egdell*, therefore, whilst the limited disclosure to the medical director of the hospital and the Home Office was justified in the public interest, a wider disclosure – say to a newspaper – could not have been justified.

Article 8 of the European Convention on Human Rights

The European Convention was effectively incorporated into English law on 2nd October 2000 when the Human Rights Act 1998 came into force. There have been several attempts to challenge law previously decided on the basis that various practices are contrary to the Convention, and, it must be said, with very limited success. As far as confidentiality is concerned, the question arises as to whether the Convention adds anything to the existing law.

Article 8 provides as follows:

1. Everyone has the right to respect for his private and family life, his home and his correspondence.

2. There shall be no interference by a public authority with the exercise of this right except such as is in accordance with the law and is necessary in a democratic society in the interest of national security, public safety or the economic well being of the country, for the prevention of disorder or crime, for the protection of health or morals, or for the protection of the rights and freedoms of others.

This article is one of the most limited in its application because of the very wide exceptions set out in paragraph two. Many of the European cases acknowledge that there has been a breach of Article 8 but then go on to find that it is justified under these exceptions. Breaches of confidentiality can, of course, be permitted under the common law, and the public interest arguments are such that they should be able to fit into the exceptions. It is arguable that the European Court of Human Rights is prepared to give a wide interpretation to the exceptions under Article 8(2), as in *MS* v *Sweden* (1997) 45 BMLR 133, where medical records relating to a woman's gynaecological condition held by a clinic had been requested by, and disclosed to, the social security department dealing with her claim for state industrial injury benefit. She had not been consulted about this, and the European Court held that this clear breach under Article 8(1), was, nevertheless, justified under Article 8(2) on the basis that the needs of the state (to avoid paying funds from the public purse to undeserving cases) were for the economic well being of the country. A European concept, which is often used to decide whether such exceptions are justifiable, is that of 'proportionality' i.e. the measure taken must not be disproportionate to that which was being protected under Article 8(2). It is arguable, however, that it is disproportionate to obtain medical records in this way, without prior reference to the claimant. A more appropriate way of achieving the same end would have been for such claims to be subject to the consent of the claimant to the disclosure of all *relevant* medical records (the case of *MS* had, at least in part, given rise to the court action because the records disclosed had contained information about a wholly irrelevant abortion).

However, there is no doubt that Article 8 is wider than the common law doctrine of confidentiality as it protects an individual's private life *per se* and not just confidential information which has been acquired in circumstances which have the necessary quality of confidentiality. An illustration of the difference is the taking of unauthorised photographs, so, for example, in the case of *Kaye* v *Robertson* (1990), *The Times* 21 March, there was found to be no cause of action when a trespassing journalist took photographs of an actor in his hospital bed, on the basis that there was then no right to privacy in English law. Article 8 would now afford protection to someone in his position, as it is highly unlikely that Article 8(2) could be invoked in support of the invasion of privacy.

Statutory provisions

As indicated above, there is some statutory protection given to certain confidential information, although the provisions often provide a statutory basis for *disclosure* in certain circumstances. For example,

The National Health Service (Venereal Diseases) Regulations 1974 (SI 1974/29) provide as follows:

Confidential of information

... Every Regional Health Authority and every District Health Authority shall take all necessary steps to secure that any information capable of identifying an individual obtained by officers of the Authority with respect to persons examined or treated for any sexually transmitted disease shall not be disclosed except:

(a) for the purpose of communicating that information to a medical practitioner or to a person employed under the direction of a medical practitioner in connection with the treatment of persons suffering from such disease or the prevention of the spread thereof; and

(b) for the purpose of such treatment or prevention.

Kennedy and Grubb[5] make the point that the words suggest that it is only information relating to the treatment and only when the GP is also treating the disease, that the exception comes into play. It should also be noted that there are regulations relating to NHS Trusts (the NHS Trusts (Venereal Disease) Directions 1991). A further point made by Kennedy and Grubb is that these regulations do not apply if the condition has been acquired other than through sexual transmission.

The Health Act 1999 created the Commission for Health Improvement (CHI), which can be authorised to inspect NHS premises and take copies of documents includes authorisation in respect of patient records. Section 23(2) limits the obtaining of such information as follows:

Section 23 (2)

Regulations under this section may not make provision with respect to the disclosure of confidential information, which relates to and identifies a living individual unless one or more of the following conditions is satisfied:–

(a) the information is disclosed in a form in which the identity of the individual cannot be ascertained;

(b) the individual consents to the information being disclosed;

---

5.   Kennedy I and Grubb A, *Medical Law*, (London: Butterworths, 2000, Third edition by Grubb, A.)

(c) the individual cannot be traced despite the taking of all reasonable steps;

(d) in a case where the Commission is exercising its functions under section 20(1)(c) (the section which relates to the Commission's function of carrying out investigations into, and making reports on, the management, provision or quality of health care for the Health Authorities, Primary Care Trusts or NHS Trusts):–

    (i) it is not practicable to disclose the information in a form in which the identity of the individual cannot be ascertained,

    (ii) the Commission considers that there is a serious risk to the health or safety of patients arising out of the matters which are the subject of the exercise of those functions, and

    (iii) having regard to that risk and the urgency of the exercise of those functions, the Commission considers that the information should be disclosed without the consent of the individual.

Similar restrictions are imposed upon the powers of the Health Service Ombudsman in respect of information obtained in the course of that function (see the Health Service Commissioner Act 1993). The Health and Social Care Act 2001 provides for very wide, some might say unacceptably wide, terms for the Secretary of State for Health to make regulations as follows:

Section 60

Control of patient information

(1) The Secretary of State may by regulations make such provision for and in connection with requiring or regulating the processing of prescribed patient information for medical purposes as he considers necessary or expedient–

    (a) in the interests of improving patient care, or
    (b) in the public interest.

Regulations may not make provision requiring the processing of confidential patient information for any purpose if it would be reasonably practicable to achieve that purpose otherwise than pursuant to such regulations, having regard to the cost of and the technology available for achieving that purpose, and neither may they make provision for requiring the processing of confidential patient information solely or principally for the purpose of determining the care and treatment to be given to particular individuals. There is provision for the Secretary of State to consult with appropriate bodies (subsection 7), and the provisions of this section are subject to the Data Protection Act 1998 (c. 29).

The Secretary of State has now issued draft regulations (The Health Service (Control of Patient Information) Regulations 2002) which provide for the creation of databases for the purposes of surveillance and analysis of health and disease, public health, occupational health and safety, and other medical purposes such as medical research. The regulations are controversial as they do make provision for disclosure of patient information which would otherwise be unlawful and where consent cannot be obtained. Although Regulation 6(2) provides that, in so far as it is practical to do so, such records should be anonymised, there is no absolute requirement to do this. As the Department of Health's Explanatory Notes suggest there is concern about this, stating that they seek to balance the need for medical research and public health measures to be undertaken and the importance of not undermining patients' rights to confidentiality. It should be noted that the Secretary of State has to give approval for the processing of such information. There is considerable disquiet at this enormous concentration of power in the Secretary of State's hands. Decisions would be amenable to judicial review, and the Secretary of State has, as required, certified that the regulations comply with the Human Rights Act 1998 i.e. that they are consistent with the provisions of the European Convention, in particular Article 8 which protects the right to privacy. It remains to be seen how effectively these safeguards will work.

It should be noted that s 18 of the Prevention of Terrorism Act 1989 created a criminal offence in respect of failure to disclose information which might be of material assistance in preventing acts of terrorism or in apprehending or securing a prosecution or conviction. When the 1989 Act was replaced with the Terrorism Act 2000 this measure was not re-enacted.

Other statutory provisions are contained within the Abortion Regulations of 1991 (SI 91/499) and the Public Health (Control of Disease) Act 1984.

The Road Traffic Act 1988 provides that a person can be required to give any information which it is in his power to give and may lead to the identification of a driver of a vehicle who may have committed a road traffic offence. This applies to health care workers (see *Hunter* v *Mann* [1974] 1 QB 767).

The Police and Criminal Evidence Act 1984, sections 9, 11 and 12, empower the police to obtain access to 'personal records' and 'human tissue or tissue fluid which has been taken for the purposes of diagnosis of medical treatment and which a person holds in confidence'. 'Personal records' includes medical records. The person(s) concerned can be dead or alive. The courts have given a wide interpretation to these provisions (see *R* v *Cardiff Crown Court ex parte Kellam* (1993) 16 BMLR 76).

A positive obligation to disclose?

The concern of this chapter, up until now, has been the justification of breaching medical confidences. However, it is arguable that there might be certain situations in which a doctor, or other health care professional, will be required to disclose, and might, for example, be successfully sued by someone who has suffered damage as a result of the failure to disclose. This situation was considered in the Californian case of *Tarasoff* v *Regents of the University of California* 17 Cal 3d 425 (1976). In that case, a patient confessed to his therapist that he had a wish to kill a fellow-student. The therapist alerted the 'campus' police to this, and they apprehended the man, interviewed him and formed the view that he was harmless. He subsequently killed the girl concerned, and her family sued the therapist because he had not warned her that she might be in danger. By a majority, the Californian Supreme Court upheld the claim. It must be noted that, here, there was a *specific* potential victim. Similarly, in the case of *Reisner* v *Regents of the University of California* (1997) Med L Rev 250, another Californian case, a doctor was found to be in breach of duty of care in not warning a sexual partner of a patient of the fact that the patient was HIV positive.

If there is no specific victim however, even if the doctor is satisfied that the patient is dangerous, generally speaking there is no duty owed (at least in English law) to the public at large. In *Palmer* v *Tees Health Authority* [1999] Lloyd's Rep Med 351 a mother sued health authorities for negligence when her four year old daughter was sexually assaulted and murdered by a psychiatric patient in their care. The child, on her way to buy ice cream, was killed by a man who had a history of child sex abuse, and who was living in a flat overlooking the road in which the mother and child lived. Although there had been a catalogue of blunders by the various authorities dealing with this man, the Court of Appeal rejected the mother's claim under the Fatal Accidents Act 1976 for the death of the child, and her own claim for psychiatric illness, because, in law, there was no cause of action. This was because there was no duty owed to the woman and her child; they were regarded as being members of the public with no special relationship of 'proximity' to the killer. It must be noted that, as is often the case where there is an allegation of negligence, particularly against public authorities, there is an element of 'policy' in such cases: warning someone against whom a specific threat has been made is one thing; issuing a warning to members of the public at large can create alarm and unrest. In order, therefore, for a claim to succeed there would have to be good evidence of a specific prior link between the attacker and the victim.

CHAPTER 2
STATUTORY PROTECTION OF MEDICAL RECORDS

David Bainbridge, Reader in Law, Aston University

Introduction

The Data Protection Act 1984 applied only to personal data that were processed automatically or were intended to be so processed. Bearing in mind that a great deal of data relating to patients is in paper form, the Data Protection Act 1998, which extended data protection law to certain types of manual files, has had a massive impact on the processing of personal data in respect of medical records. Furthermore, the 1998 Act expressly classifies 'health' data (personal data consisting of information as to an individual's physical or mental health or condition) as sensitive personal data and imposes, expressly and impliedly, stricter controls over the processing of such data.

Although the Access to Health Records Act 1990 gave a right of access to medical records, whether in electronic or paper form, the Data Protection Act 1998 is of much wider scope and, with the Statutory Instruments made under that Act, sets out a complete framework both regulating the processing of all forms of personal data and providing for comprehensive rights for individuals. Of course, like any area of law, the data protection law draws from numerous sources additional to the specific legislation and associated case law directed at data protection. For example, the law of breach of confidence may be relevant in some cases as may be copyright law and the recently introduced database right. Even the laws of defamation and malicious falsehood may be relevant in rare cases. The Health and Social Care Act 2001 gives the Secretary of State the power to provide additional and more specific restrictions on the use of information relating to patients, without derogating from the protection afforded by the Data Protection Act 1998.

Another, very important source of law is the European Convention on Human Rights and Fundamental Freedoms, brought into English law by the Human Rights Act 1998 with its twin and sometimes contradictory rights of privacy and freedom of expression. The extent to which the Data Protection Act 1998 complies with, or is inconsistent with, the Convention remains to be seen though two points can be made at this stage. The 'Data Protection Directive', which was implemented in the United Kingdom by the Data Protection Act 1998, was drafted with an eye on the European Convention on Human Rights and Fundamental Freedoms. Secondly, the Human Rights Act 1998 provides for the resolution of conflicts between the Convention and inconsistent domestic law to be resolved in favour of the Convention.

Individuals' rights and freedoms flowing from a general right to privacy deserve special treatment in respect of processing medical data of a personal nature. There are many dangers associated with such processing. For example, unauthorised disclosure or loss of such data could have serious consequences as could inaccuracies in health data. There are serious concerns about the processing of personal data indicating that a patient is terminally ill or suffering from AIDS. Genetic data are another potential minefield. Apart from basic privacy issues, the thought of such data falling into the 'wrong hands' is very worrying and security of electronic and paper-based medical data should be at a very high level.

Rights of privacy are not just passive and data protection law gives individuals rights to interfere with processing activity in some cases together with rights to require the provision of information about processing activity together with a right of access to their personal data. The creation of new rights for individuals and the enhancement of their previous rights under data protection law should not be overlooked. A further factor is that individuals are becoming better informed about their rights and are more prepared to exercise them.

Other issues associated with the processing of health data are:

- collecting data and informing patients of the identity of the data controller and the purposes of processing (and further information to ensure processing is fair),

- secondary uses, for example, for research or statistical analysis,

- retention, for example, to defend potential claims for negligence or to provide information to individuals contemplating legal action for personal injury where the injuries were treated by a hospital (for example, X-rays showing the gravity of the injury),

- security and processing personal data by contractors,

- patients' access to data including X-rays and scans,

- disclosures and transfers of data, for example, where a patient is going to Europe for treatment,

This chapter will focus on the impact of data protection law in the context of medical records, referring to other legislation and areas of law where appropriate. Before looking at specific issues relating to medical records, the background to the Data Protection Act 1998 and the basic framework it provides for the processing of personal data are discussed.

Background to the Act

Directive 95/46/EC of the European Parliament and of the Council of Europe 24 October 1995 on the Protection of Individuals with regard to the Processing of Personal Data and on the Free Movement of Such Data (OJ L281, 23.11.95, p31) (the 'Data Protection Directive') was a response, in part, to the potential for barriers to be erected to the freedom of movement of personal data within Europe resulting from disparities between Member States in the level of protection of personal data. The approach used in the Directive was to harmonise data protection law at a relatively high level throughout Europe (the Directive has effect in the European Economic Area which includes the 15 Member States of the EU together with Liechtenstein, Iceland and Norway). Consequently, no single State would be able to object to the transfer of personal data from that State to any other EEA State solely on the ground of disparity in protection for personal data.

The importance of the European Convention on Human Rights and Fundamental Freedoms is clear from the recitals to the Directive. In recital 1, one of the objectives of the European Community is declared to be the promotion of:

> ... democracy on the basis of the fundamental rights recognized in the constitution and laws of the Member States and in the European Convention for the Protection of Human Rights and Fundamental Freedoms

Recital 10 goes on to state that the approximation of national data protection laws must not lessen the protection conferred by the Convention but must, on the contrary, seek to ensure a high level of protection throughout the Community.

Nevertheless, the Directive (as a proposal in 1992) was met with some hostility, particularly in the United Kingdom and the Netherlands. In the United Kingdom, the National Health Service reckoned it would cost in excess of £1 billion in the first year alone as the new law would require every individual to give express consent to the processing of his or her personal data by the NHS.[1] A study carried out by the CBI for the Home Office produced a cost of implementing the Directive in the order of £2.3 billion for the 625 organisations partaking in the study. In practice, these fears of the financial consequences of the new law appear to have been somewhat exaggerated.

A Data Protection Bill intended to implement the Directive was introduced in the House of Lords on 14 January 1998, following a White Paper.[2] There were a number of amendments in the Lords and the Bill was introduced in the House of Commons in March 1998 where further amendments were made. Royal Assent was received on 16 July 1998. Although compliance with the Directive was required by 24 October 1998, the major provisions of the new Act did not come into force until 1 March 2000. With the exception of section 56 which makes certain forms of enforced subject access an offence, all of the Act was in force by that date.

Certainly, the new Act made some far-reaching changes to data protection law and has significant cost implications for data controllers in all sectors. The financial memorandum to the Bill gave some estimates. Start up costs were estimated at £194m for government (central and local), £836m for the private sector and £120m for the voluntary sector. Annual recurring costs were estimated at less but were still put at £630m for the private sector.

---

1.   Department of Health, "Draft EC Directive on Data Protection: Analysis of Costs," 1994.
2.   Home Office, *Data Protection: The Government's Proposals*, 1997, Cm 3725.

The complexity of the new law was demonstrated by the number of amendments made during the passage of the Bill through Parliament and the making of at least one statutory instrument which can only be explained on the basis that it provided for additional allowable forms of processing that had not been picked up earlier. This includes the provision of data relating to parents, siblings and other relatives to insurance companies without those persons' express consent (for example, when completing a life assurance proposal form where questions are asked about the health of such persons) and processing data relating to religion or disabilities for the purposes of equal opportunity monitoring.

Framework of Data Protection under the 1998 Act

The Data Protection Act 1998 sets out a model of data protection law based on relationships between the various persons involved. These relationships represent rights, duties and powers as the case may be. Before looking at the mechanics of data protection, it is worth reflecting on the identity of the various persons involved in data protection law.

Note that some of the definitions in the Act are very technical and the following descriptions are simplified in some cases. For a fully detailed exposition of the Act see *Bainbridge*.[3]

Data controller:
The person who determines the purposes and manner of processing.

Data subject:
The individual to whom the personal data relate.

Information Commissioner:
The supervisory authority in the United Kingdom responsible for enforcing data protection and with a number of other roles including maintaining the register of data controllers, raising awareness of data protection, consultation and advising on data protection.

Processor:
A person who processes personal data on behalf of the data controller (but not including an employee of the data controller).

---

3.   Bainbridge D I, *Data Protection Law* (EMIS Professional Publishing, 2000).

Recipient:
A person to whom personal data are disclosed (including an employee or agent of either the data controller or a processor).

Third party:
Anyone other than a data subject, a data controller, processor or anyone (such as an employee or agent) authorised to process the data on behalf of either a data controller of a processor. Third parties to whom data are disclosed will also be recipients.

Being able to classify persons according to these definitions is important in a number of ways. For example, data controllers may only process personal data as allowed by the Data Protection Act 1998 and are required to notify their processing activities to the Information Commissioner, to the extent that they are not covered by exemptions. They are also bound to data subjects by a number of duties imposed on them. Processors must be subject to the same security obligations as data controllers which must be imposed contractually, being in writing or evidenced in writing. Information as to the identity of recipients must be included in any notification to the Information Commissioner (though only in a generic form) and disclosures to third parties may trigger a duty to inform data subjects as to the identity of the third party and the purposes of processing to be carried out by the third party. In some cases, the ability to process personal data may depend on whether the data subject's consent has been obtained. Implied consent may suffice where the data are non-sensitive but in the case of sensitive personal data, such as the sort of data found in medical records, nothing less than informed and express consent will do. The Act requires 'explicit consent' but the Directive is quite clear that it must be unambiguous and informed consent where the personal data are sensitive. From the perspective of the author's experiences, health professionals consistently fail to satisfy this requirement adequately.

Figure 1 shows the various persons affected by data protection law and the relationships, rights and duties between them.

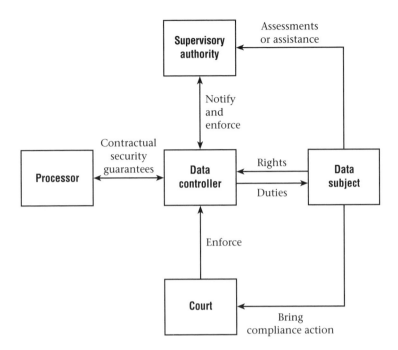

Figure 1. The mechanics of data protection

The key to data protection law is the concept of transparency. Individuals should know or be able to discover without undue effort, who is processing personal data relating to them and the purposes of such processing. This important principle has been emasculated by the notification process adopted in the United Kingdom. This is because it is possible to notify recipients by using generic terms such as 'suppliers', 'retail organisations' and 'advisors'. It is highly arguable that this means that the United Kingdom has failed to comply with the spirit of the Directive. However, the first data protection principle requires that processing be fair and lawful and the first limb of this requires that data subjects are made aware of any use of their personal data not apparent at the time the data were first obtained from them.[3]

---

3. *Innovations (Mail Order) Ltd* v *Data Protection Registrar*, 29 September 1993, Data Protection Tribunal, under the 1984 Act in which it was held that data subjects should be informed of, and consent to, non-obvious uses at the time the data were collected from the data subject.

To understand the scope of data protection law under the 1998 Act, some of the other definitions in the Act are important. In particular, the definition of *processing* is very wide and means:

> ... obtaining, recording or holding the information or data or carrying out any operation or set of operations on the information or data, including–
>
> (a) organisation, adaptation or alteration of the information or data,
>
> (b) retrieval, consultation or use of the information or data,
>
> (c) disclosure of the information or data by transmission, dissemination or otherwise making available, or
>
> (d) alignment, combination, blocking, erasure or destruction of the information or data.

The operations listed are not exhaustive and it should be noted that the inclusion of 'holding' implies that simply being in possession of data is caught and the language of the Directive makes this even clearer. As there is a requirement that processors are subject to the same obligations as data controllers as regards security (which must be imposed contractually) this has far reaching implications. For example, contractors carrying out IT functions, disaster recovery services or even disposal of old computer print-out must be adequately supervised in this respect and appropriate terms must be incorporated into contracts with them.

What types of data are within data protection law?

The Data Protection Act 1998 applies to:

- data which are being processed by automatic means (or where there is an intention to process the data automatically),

- 'relevant filing systems' (structured manual files permitted easy access to specific data relating to one or more individuals) and

- accessible records, which include certain health records.

Thus, health data held on computer are within the Act, as are health data included in structured manual files (relevant filing systems) and as are unstructured manual files containing health data (accessible records). An example of the latter might be a file containing a letter of referral to a consultant made by a general practitioner and a hand-written or typed record of the consultation and findings. If the record is entered on a pro-forma, then the record will be a relevant filing system. In other words, where health data are concerned there is no escaping the full rigours of data protection law. This is not the case in some other walks of life, for example, in relation to files that are not structured and where the data are not health data (or in educational or accessible public records as defined in the Act). For example, a general correspondence file containing letters and memos is not within the meaning of data for the purposes of the Act, unless it contains data relating to health, educational or accessible public records.

As mentioned earlier, the main provisions of the Access to Health Records Act 1990, which previously gave a right of access to *manual* health records as the Data Protection Act 1984 only applied to *automated* processing, have been subsumed in the 1998 Act. The remaining rump of the 1990 Act deals primarily with requests for access on behalf of deceased persons (the Data Protection Act 1998 only applies to living individuals).

Although the Data Protection Act 1998 carries a definition of data it is neutral as to the types of information that are incorporated in the data. The Directive is more helpful and makes it clear that it is not restricted to text and covers image data and aural data. Recital 14 to the Directive states that it should apply to the processing of sound and image data, given the importance of technical developments in the capture, transmission, manipulation, recording, storing or communication of such data. The key is whether an individual can be identified from the data (or from the data and other information in the possession of or likely to come into the possession of the data controller). Thus, in a health care context, data protection law applies to x-rays, scans, recordings of ultrasound and infrasound tests, blood and urine tests, biopsies, graphs or charts showing temperature, blood pressure, electro-cardiograph readouts, etc just as much as it applies to information such as doctors' notes, diagnoses, treatment regimes and prescription details.

The Data Protection Act 1998 states processing cannot be carried out unless one of the conditions in Schedule 2 to the Act applies or, in the case of sensitive personal data, one of the conditions in Schedule 3 is met *additionally*. This derives from the first data protection principle which stipulates that processing must be fair and lawful.

The distinction between 'normal' personal data and sensitive personal data is, therefore, of some import. 'Normal' personal data are not defined but sensitive personal data are personal data consisting of information as to:

(a) the racial or ethnic origin of the data subject,

(b) his political opinions,

(c) his religious or other beliefs of a similar nature,

(d) whether he is a member of a trade union ...,

(e) his physical or mental health or condition,

(f) his sexual life,

(g) the commission or alleged commission by him of any offence, or

(h) any proceedings for any offence committed or alleged to have been committed by him, the disposal of such proceedings or the sentence of any court in such proceedings.

Clearly much of the data processed by health professionals will be sensitive personal data as it will relate directly to physical or mental health or condition but other data may also be processed in connection with health care. For example, race or ethnic data may be recorded in a case of sickle cell anaemia and religious beliefs data may be collected where relevant to diet (for example in relation to an Islamic patient) or to the acceptability of blood transfusions (for example, in the case of a Jehovah's witness). The implications of processing sensitive personal data will be examined later in this Chapter.

The Data Protection Principles

The data protection principles have already been alluded to. They lie at the heart of data protection law and most of them derive directly from the European Convention on Data Protection (Convention for the Protection of Individuals with Regard to Automatic Processing of Personal Data, Strasbourg, 28.1.1981).[5] There are eight principles, as follows:

1. Personal data shall be processed fairly and lawfully and, in particular, shall not be processed unless–

    (a) at least one of the conditions in Schedule 2 is met, and

    (b) in the case of sensitive personal data, at least one of the conditions in Schedule 3 is also met.

2. Personal data shall be obtained only for one or more specified and lawful purposes, and shall not be further processed in any manner incompatible with that purpose or those purposes.

3. Personal data shall be adequate, relevant and not excessive in relation to the purpose or purposes for which they are processed.

4. Personal data shall be accurate and, where necessary, kept up to date.

5. Personal data processed for any purpose or purposes shall not be kept for longer than is necessary for that purpose or those purposes.

6. Personal data shall be processed in accordance with the rights of data subjects under this Act.

7. Appropriate technical and organisational measures shall be taken against unauthorised or unlawful processing of personal data and against accidental loss or destruction of, or damage to, personal data.

8. Personal data shall not be transferred to a country or territory outside the European Economic Area unless that country or territory ensures an adequate level of protection for the rights and freedoms of data subjects in relation to the processing of personal data.

The Act contains some interpretation of these principles.

---

5. See full text @
    http://conventions.coe.int/treaty/EN/WhatYouWant.asp?NT=108&CU=8&DF=.

First Data Protection Principle

For processing to be fair, factors to be taken into account include the method of obtaining the data and whether the person from whom they were obtained was deceived or misled as to the purpose or purposes of processing. The first principle also imposes obligations of data controllers to inform data subjects. Typically this requires the provision of information as to the identity of the data controller and the purpose or purposes of the processing. Further information may be required to be given to ensure that the processing is fair. This would include information about any processing activity that is not obvious to the individual concerned. If the data are intended to be used subsequently for a purpose beyond the immediate treatment and care of the patient, he or she should be told this at the outset and given an opportunity to object. An example is where the data will be used for research or statistics in such a manner that the data subject can still be identified from the data.[6] The alternative requires that the data subject is informed before such secondary processing commences. In many cases, this will be exceptionally onerous to comply with (but see later under the second principle).

Where the data have not been collected directly from the data subject, there is still an obligation to inform the data subject as to the identity of the data controller, the purposes of processing and any other information so as to make the processing fair. However, in this case, the obligation is not absolute and does not apply where the disclosure is required under a legal obligation (other than a contractual obligation) or where to comply would result in a disproportionate effort and the data controller records his reasons for believing this is so at the time. A further requirement is that the data subject has not notified the data controller in writing that he or she should be provided with information in the case of subsequent processing by third parties. Whilst disproportionate effort may be relevant when processing personal data relating to large numbers of data subjects it should be noted that this exemption from providing information does not apply in respect of subsequent processing by the data controller who obtained the data from the data subject in the first place.

A further point is that the obligation to provide information as to the purposes of processing can be satisfied by notification of the processing activity to the Information Commissioner. In this way, the information is publicly available and the data controller can be taken to have complied with this requirement. However, there remains the obligation

---

6.   Under Schedule 8 of the Data Protection Act 1998, an exemption that applies to historical research does not excuse the data controller from the obligations associated with informing the data subject.

to provide information as to the identity of the data controller and any further information to ensure that the processing is fair.

Manual processing is not required to be notified under the Data Protection Act 1998 and there are further exceptions, such as in the case of processing for accounts and records, advertising, marketing and public relations, staff administration and certain forms of processing by non-profit-making organisations. These exceptions are fairly narrow and strictly relate to the particular purpose.

Exemption from notification has two implications. First, there is a duty to provide information broadly equivalent to that which would have been included in a notification to the Information Commissioner within 21 days to any person making a written request. Secondly, by notifying processing exempt from the requirement to notify, the data controller is excused from providing information as to the purposes of processing to data subjects. The Information Commissioner has made it clear that processing exempt from notification may still be included in a notification under the Act. As a great deal of processing in the context of health care is manual processing, data controllers such as NHS Trusts, GP surgeries and the like ought to consider notifying all their manual processing also.

Second and Fifth Data Protection Principles

Personal data are not to be further processed in a manner incompatible with the purpose or purposes for which they were originally obtained. This suggests that processing health data for research or statistical analysis at some future date will fall foul of this principle unless the data subject was informed at the time the data were collected, or at some later time, that such processing was likely in the future. However, the Data Protection Act 1998 provides an exemption for processing for research purposes (this is taken to include statistical and historical purposes) where the data are not processed to support measures or decisions with respect to particular individuals and are not processed in such a way as to cause, or be likely to cause, substantial damage or substantial distress to any data subject. Where this applies the processing is not deemed to be contrary to the second data protection principle.

Research data may be kept for long periods of time. Therefore, processing for research purposes in accordance with the above conditions may be kept indefinitely, notwithstanding the fifth data protection principle.

In most cases, data used for research will be anonymous, having all personal identifiers removed from the data. Providing the individuals cannot subsequently be identified (either because of other information in the hands of the data controller or a third party or because the data are unique and can readily be associated with a particular individual). This means that such data are outside the provisions of the Data Protection Act 1998. Data as to patients' drug prescriptions from which personal identifiers had been removed was held to be outside the protection of the Act and, furthermore, it was held that the patients did not 'own' such data so as to prevent its subsequent disclosure by doctors and pharmacists for research purposes on the basis of a breach of confidence.[7]

The fifth data protection principle is also relevant in the context of the retention of data for purposes associated with defending legal actions, for example, in respect of allegations of medical negligence. The retention of medical data may also be important where an ex-patient wishes to sue a third party for personal injury and a doctor or hospital has data such as X-rays which can be used to assess the gravity of the injury and the longer term prognosis. This could be particularly important in assessing damages for future loss of earnings and expenses resulting from loss of mobility, for example.

Data should not be kept for longer than is necessary for the purpose or purposes of processing. There is no interpretative guidance in the Act as to the fifth principle and no specific exemption from this principle for the purposes of defending legal actions or providing evidence for legal proceedings. This means, therefore, that such purposes must be included in any notification to the Information Commissioner under the Act unless another notified purpose justifies keeping the data for a sufficient period of time. Indeed, destroying medical records too quickly could prejudice the rights and freedoms of data subjects.

Seventh Data Protection Principle

The seventh data protection principle, imposing security obligations on data controllers, requires consideration to be given to a number of factors, being the state of technological development and the costs of implementing security measures. Regard has to be given to the harm

---

7.   R v *Department of Health, ex parte Source Informatics Ltd* [2001] FSR 8.

that might result from unauthorised or unlawful processing, accidental loss, destruction or damage and the nature of the data. Clearly with health data the risks of unauthorised or unlawful processing are very great, for example, where data are disclosed to someone not entitled to have access to them. Loss or destruction could also be a serious matter, for example, where the data indicate an allergic reaction to a particular drug.

The data controller has to take reasonable steps to ensure that employees having access to personal data are reliable and must choose data processors which provide sufficient guarantees with respect to technical and organisational security measures. Furthermore, the data controller must ensure that those measures are complied with, implying some degree of supervision and the processor's obligations must be imposed by contractual means and be in writing or evidenced in writing. The contract must require the processor only to act on the data controller's instructions and impose obligations equivalent to those imposed on the data controller by the seventh data protection principle. Bearing in mind the very wide meaning of processing, particular care is needed in relation to agency staff, contractors operating the data controller's IT facilities or providing back-up services and even contractors engaged to remove and destroy old medical records.

Eighth Data Protection Principle

Part of the rationale underlying the Data Protection Directive was to ensure the freedom of movement of personal data within Europe. Therefore, providing the processing is still within the data protection principles, transfers of personal data within the European Economic Area may proceed without hindrance. This may be important, for example, in the context of patients resident in the United Kingdom who are sent to hospitals in other European countries for treatment, such as Germany and France.

In the context of health care, transfers of personal data to countries outside the European Economic Area will be relatively rare. The eighth principle prohibits transfers to third countries (countries or territories outside the European Economic Area) that do not have adequate protection for personal data in respect of the transfer envisaged. Nonetheless, in a bold act of pragmatism, transfers of personal data may yet proceed providing one of the conditions in Schedule 4 is met. These include the data subject's consent, where the transfer is in connection with a contract with the data subject, where the vital interests of the data subject are concerned or if the transfer is governed by contractual terms or is otherwise in a manner so as to provide adequate safeguards for the rights and freedoms of data subjects.

Conditions for processing

The first data protection principle does not allow processing unless at least one of the conditions in Schedule 2 to the Act is met and, where the data are sensitive personal data, at least one of the conditions in Schedule 3 is also met.

The conditions in Schedule 2 most relevant in a health context are where the data subject has given his consent to the processing, where processing is necessary in the performance of a contract with the data subject (or preliminary to such a contract), where the data controller is under a legal obligation to carry out the processing or in respect of 'legitimate interests' processing. This latter condition will be relevant in a great many cases and applies where the processing is necessary for the legitimate interests pursued by the data controller or a third party to whom the data are disclosed except where the processing is unwarranted in any particular case by reason of prejudice to the rights and freedoms or legitimate interests of the data subject.

Three points can be made about legitimate interests processing. First, the word necessary should be taken in a weak sense. Secondly, 'legitimate interests' probably means interests that are not unlawful (whether in the sense of data protection law or other laws) and should be something which is not *ultra vires* in respect of the data controller's organisation's powers. The third point to note is that the condition may require a balance to be struck between the interests of the data controller and those of data subjects.[8]

Processing in the context of a contract will be relevant where a patient is undergoing private health care but, of course, this alone only allows processing of non-sensitive personal data, such as name, address, gender and age.

Where the personal data are sensitive data, a further condition must be satisfied before processing can be undertaken. One of the conditions

---

8.   Balancing of interests was accepted as a proper approach to legitimate interests processing by the European Court of Justice in *R* v *Minister of Agriculture, Fisheries and Food, ex parte Fisher, The Times*, 10 October 2000.

from Schedule 3 must apply in addition to one in Schedule 2. The conditions in Schedule 3 relevant to health care are:

- that the data subject has given his explicit consent to the processing;

- where the processing is necessary in order to protect the vital interests of the data subject or another person, in a case where consent cannot be given by or on behalf of the data subject, or the data controller cannot reasonably be expected to obtain the consent of the data subject, or in order to protect the vital interests of another person, in a case where consent by or on behalf of the data subject has been unreasonably withheld;

- where the processing is necessary for the purpose of, or in connection with, any legal proceedings (including prospective legal proceedings), is necessary for the purpose of obtaining legal advice, or is otherwise necessary for the purposes of establishing, exercising or defending legal rights;

- where the processing is necessary for medical purposes and is undertaken by a health professional, or a person who in the circumstances owes a duty of confidentiality which is equivalent to that which would arise if that person were a health professional.

In respect of the last condition, 'medical purposes' includes the purposes of preventative medicine, medical diagnosis, medical research, the provision of care and treatment and the management of healthcare services.

Processing sensitive personal data for the purpose of equal opportunity and treatment monitoring is also allowed where the data relate to race or ethnic origin, religious beliefs or other beliefs of a similar nature or physical or mental health or condition.

In many cases, patients will be in a position to give express consent. However, it may not be enough simply to ask the patient to sign a consent form as the Directive makes it clear that the consent should be informed consent (consent is defined in the Directive in terms of being a freely given, specific and informed indication of the data subject's wishes signifying agreement to the processing of the personal data). Therefore, there should be some explanation of the purposes of processing envisaged at the time the data are collected from the patient. In any case, and notwithstanding that one of the other conditions for processing sensitive personal data might be relied on instead, such as processing for medical purposes, the data subject should be given information concerning the purposes of processing where not absolutely obvious, otherwise, the processing will not comply with the first data protection principle.

Fair Processing

The concept of fair processing is an all-embracing principle that requires that the data subject is aware of the purposes for which his or her personal data will be used, direct or indirect, actual or potential, with few exceptions. In terms of future uses, it may be acceptable to postpone giving information to the data subject but there should be a cost-free opportunity for the data subject to object before the processing is underway. Where disclosure to a third party triggers the duty to inform data subjects, although in principle the data controller may be able to rely on disproportionate effort to avoid this duty, it is submitted that to do so in connection with sensitive health data would be to fall foul of the first data protection principle.

'Vital interests' processing might apply, for example, where a person in urgent need of medical treatment is unconscious or otherwise unable to give consent. This will allow disclosure of information such as blood group, drugs currently being taken, etc. The condition allows processing where consent is unreasonably withheld or where it is impracticable to obtain consent. Where such situations arise, it will be sensible for a record to be kept of reasons why this condition is thought to apply.

Defending legal claims and responding to legal processing is something that has become all to familiar in relation to health care. This allows, for example, a hospital or general practitioner's surgery to retain health data that may be important in connection with claims for negligence. However, consideration must also be given to the fifth data protection principle, discussed above. Although the Limitation Act 1980 places a long stop of three years when a legal action may be commenced in respect of personal injury or death, there are a number of exceptions, such as where the claimant could not reasonably be expected to know of the negligent treatment or diagnosis for some time. In some cases, a patient may not be aware of the injury caused by negligence for a number of years. Although the basic rule is that the time runs from the date the injury was sustained, it may run from the date the injured person first knows of the injury, if this is later. A number of factors may be relevant in deciding whether a later date may be used, including the nature of any symptoms or other indicators, the extent to which they were paid attention to, whether they were such to put the person on notice that something was wrong and whether it was reasonable for the person to have sought expert advice.[9]

The condition relating to medical purposes is very wide, especially when the definition of 'health professional' is considered. It is given by section 69 of the Data Protection Act 1998 as any of the following:

(a) a registered medical practitioner,

(b) a registered dentist as defined by section 53(1) of the Dentists Act 1984,

(c) a registered optician as defined by section 36(1) of the Opticians Act 1989,

(d) a registered pharmaceutical chemist as defined by section 24(1) of the Pharmacy Act 1954 or a registered person as defined by Article 2(2) of the Pharmacy (Northern Ireland) Order 1976,

(e) a registered nurse, midwife or health visitor,

(f) a registered osteopath as defined by section 41 of the Osteopaths Act 1993,

(g) a registered chiropractor as defined by section 43 of the Chiropractors Act 1994,

(h) any person who is registered as a member of a profession to which the Professions Supplementary to Medicine Act 1960 for the time being extends,

(i) a clinical psychologist, child psychotherapist or speech therapist,

(j) a music therapist employed by a health service body, and

(k) a scientist employed by such a body as head of a department.

---

9.   *Nash v Eli Lilly* [1993] 1 WLR 782

In effect, the scope is even wider and can apply where the practitioner is not included in the above list providing that he or she is under a duty of confidence equivalent to that owed by a health professional.

In many cases, processing for medical purposes will be carried out on the basis of the patient's consent but where this is not so, it may be dangerous to rely on the medical purposes condition for processing. The data controller should still decide whether the processing is otherwise fair and lawful. The first data protection principle states that processing cannot be undertaken unless a condition in Schedule 2 applies and, for sensitive personal data, also at least one of the conditions in Schedule 3 is met. Satisfying this requirement does not automatically mean, however, that the processing is fair and lawful. The language of the first principle and the interpretation on it in Part II of Schedule 1 make it clear that processing may not be fair even if the conditions are met and the processing complies with the interpretative provisions on that principle. That is why informed consent is so important to data processing.

Thus, even if the medical purposes condition clearly applies, the processing may yet be unfair because the patient has not been supplied with appropriate information as to the purposes of processing. Where the data are caught by the Data Protection Act 1998, the old approach of medical practitioners of volunteering minimal information and only divulging further information in response to specific questions from the patient, is no longer tenable.

Data subjects rights

Apart from the extension of data protection law to certain types of manual files, the rights of data subjects are significantly enlarged and enhanced compared to the rights under the 1984 Act. In particular, there are new rights, being a right to prevent processing likely to cause substantial damage or substantial distress, a right to prevent processing for purposes of direct marketing, and rights in relation to automated decision-taking. However, in the context of this book it is the data subject's right of access that is of greatest import.

Right of Access

Individuals tend to exercise their right of access not out of idle curiosity but for a particular purpose, typically when they think their personal data are inaccurate or in preparation for a claim for negligence, for example, to determine whether there is likely to have been negligent diagnosis or treatment and to secure evidence of the alleged negligence or in respect of a personal injury claim against a third party.

The Data Protection Act 1998 increased the amount of information which has to be furnished by data controllers in response to subject access requests. The information to be given to the data subject is:

- whether any data relating to the data subject are being processed by or on behalf of the data controller and, if so, the data controller must:

    – give a description of the personal data;

    – the purposes for which they are being or are to be processed; and

    – the recipients or classes of recipients to whom they are or may be disclosed;

- communication to the data subject in an intelligible form – accompanied with an explanation if necessary, of:

    – the information constituting the personal data (a copy in permanent form unless this is not possible or would require a disproportionate effort or if the data subject agrees otherwise);

    – any available information as to the source of the data; and

    – a description of the logic of any automated decision-taking.

The Data Protection (Subject Access) (Fees and Miscellaneous Provisions) Regulations 2000 provide that a request for any of the above information, except in respect of a description of the logic in any automated decision-taking, is to be taken as extending to the other information to be given. A request for information as to the logic in automated decision-taking will be limited to that unless there is an express intention requiring that the other information is to be given.

The data controller can refuse to comply with subsequent identical or similar requests for subject access by a particular individual unless a reasonable interval has elapsed since the previous request. In determining what a reasonable interval is, regard shall be had to the nature of the data, the purposes of the processing and the frequency with which the data are altered. The information to be given must be as it was when the request was received apart from deletions or amendments that would have existed notwithstanding the request.

Particularly with some forms of personal data, such as health data, the data will contain information about a third party. For example, a medical report will identify the person making the report and the name of any consultant to whom the patient may be referred. In such a case, the data controller must be satisfied that the other person has consented to the disclosure of his or her personal data to the person making the request or, where it is reasonable in all the circumstances, to comply without the consent of the other. In determining whether it is reasonable in all the circumstances to comply without the consent of the other, factors that may be taken into account are any duty of confidentiality owed to the other, any steps taken by the data controller to gain the consent of the other, whether the other is capable of giving consent and any express refusal of consent by the other individual.[10]

In other cases, lack of consent does not excuse a data controller complying with the subject access request where he can provide the information without disclosing the identity of the other individual, for example, by omitting the name or other identifying particulars in a computer printout or by photocopying a manual file with the third party identifiers masked.

The general rule is that subject access must be complied with no longer than 40 days after receipt of the request (there is a shorter period for credit reference agencies and some differences to the subject access provisions in such cases). The maximum fee that can be charged is £10 but there are some differences for health records (and educational records).

Where the request for subject access relates wholly or partly to personal data forming part of a health record and the request is not restricted to data processed or intended to be processed automatically only, the maximum fee is £50 where the data subject is provided with a permanent copy of the data. Originally, this was a transitional

---

10.   These provisions were introduced to comply with the decision of the European Court on Human Rights in the case of *Gaskin* v *United Kingdom* (1990) 12 EHRR 36 where social records identifying social workers were withheld from the data subject on the grounds that the social workers objected or could not be traced. Only those records in respect of which the social workers agreed to disclosure were disclosed.

provision, reflecting the high cost of making copies of some health data such as X-rays, scans and tissue samples and it was intended that the maximum fee would be reduced to £10 from 24 October 2001. However, because of the growing number of subject access requests in respect of health data, it has been decided to keep the £50 maximum until a final resolution of the problem of high costs incurred by data controllers complying with such requests; the Data Protection (Subject Access) (Fees and Miscellaneous Provisions) (Amendment) Regulations 2001. A number of issues have been identified as leading to an increase of requests for access to health data, being:

- the consolidation of the provisions of the Access to Health Records Act 1990 relating to living individuals into the Data Protection Act 1998;

- the setting of the maximum fee that may be charged for giving access to medical records at £50 during the first transitional period under the Act (that is, until 24 October 2001, now extended);

- the development of conditional fee arrangements in litigation (so called "No Win, No Fee" litigation) and an associated increase in personal injuries claims;

- an increased awareness of data subject rights across society.[11]

One possible solution would be to allow a data controller to charge more for providing copies of X-rays and other data that are costly to copy. There are concerns, however, that this could be contrary to the Data Protection Directive which requires subject access at reasonable intervals and without excessive delay or expense.

The debate about access to medical records has been insufficiently informed by some of the provisions of the Data Protection Act itself. Section 8(2) of the Act requires that the data subject is furnished with a permanent copy of the data unless making a copy is impossible or would involve a disproportionate effort or where the data subject agrees otherwise. It is arguable that providing copies that are expensive to make, such as X-rays, would be to involve a disproportionate effort and the data controller might be deemed to comply simply by letting the data subject have a look at the data, providing an explanation is given to make the data intelligible, if necessary.

11.   Information Commissioner, *Subject Access and Medical Records: Fees for Access*, (Guidance Note, 7 November 2001, available at *www.dataprotection.gov.uk*).

Of course, many requests for access to medical records are a forerunner of potential litigation, whether against a hospital or health professional in respect of an allegation of medical negligence or to obtain evidence for possible personal injury claim against a third party, or in negotiation of a settlement in such a claim. In such circumstances, it may be reasonable to expect the data subject to pay the full cost of providing permanent copies. However, until such time as we have amending legislation dealing with the above issues, or clarification by case law, it seems more likely than not that data controllers ought to hand over permanent copies. Refusal to do so is likely to trigger a legal challenge. A failure to comply with any of the provisions relating to subject access may result in a court order to do so.

There are a number of exemptions to the subject access provisions. In terms of health data, there is an exception in relation to information about human fertilisation and embryology; Data Protection (Miscellaneous Subject Access Exemptions) Order 2000. However, the most notable exception is provided by the Data Protection (Subject Access Modification) (Health) Order 2000. This exemption applies to a situation where disclosure of information to the data subject would be likely to cause serious harm to the physical or mental health or condition of the data subject or any other person. This could be the case, for example, where a patient has a terminal illness and a health professional considers that informing the patient of this fact would be seriously detrimental to the patient. The exemption only applies to the extent that access would be likely to cause the harm referred to and there are complex provisions to deal with the situation where the data controller is not a health professional. Basically, in such a case, there is a duty to consult with a health professional.[12]

A final provision concerning health records is that, under section 57 of the Data Protection Act 1998, any term or condition in a contract is void in as much as it purports to require the supply of a record, copy or part of a record consisting of information contained in any health record. This extends also to a requirement to produce the same to another person.

It should be noted that there are further provisions dealing with subject access in other cases which are outside the scope of this book.

---

12.   See Bainbridge *op cit* at pp. 170–173.

Summary

The incorporation of those parts of the Access to Health Records Act 1990 concerning living individuals into the Data Protection Act 1998 has heightened awareness of this area of law amongst individuals. Other areas of law may also have an impact on data protection in relation to medical records, such as the European Convention on Human Rights and Fundamental Freedoms and the Freedom of Information Act 2000 which applies to all manual data, whether or not in a medical record.

There is no doubt that data controllers in the health service are placed in an onerous position when it comes to complying with data protection law. Particular issues arise from the relationship they have with data subjects which include duties to inform data subjects and to comply with data subject access requests, which can be significantly more costly to observe than the maximum £50 fee that can be charged. Other burdens include the constraints on processing and disclosures and the need for appropriate levels of security, including the contractual imposition of equivalent obligations on processors.

With the health service in the United Kingdom creaking on its hinges, resulting in the treatment of some patients in hospitals in other European countries, at least there are no barriers on the transfers of patient information to hospitals and medical practitioners in those countries, providing the data protection principles are complied with, including a duty to inform the patient accordingly. Transfers of personal data to countries outside the European Economic Area are a different matter however and, where the destination country does not have adequate protection for personal data in a particular case, in most cases, there will be a need to incorporate specific safeguards.

Data protection law under the 1998 Act still requires much clarification, which can only come through further legislation and case law, informed by experiences under the 1998 Act and other legislation impacting on data protection. But the United Kingdom cannot act unilaterally except in accordance with the Data Protection Directive and the Human Rights Convention. What makes matters worse is that the complex issues and problems faced by the health service are echoed in other sectors, such as social services, education, commerce and local and central government, all of which have their own particular burdens and priorities. However, it must not be forgotten that one of the twin aims of data protection law is to secure individuals' rights and freedoms in respect of data processing, in particular, their right of privacy. Whilst this implies some balance should be achieved between data controllers and individuals, the rights and freedoms of the individuals must be paramount. To this end, processing activities must be transparent so that individuals are aware of such activities supplemented by a right to easily and inexpensively see the detail of it and to take effective action should the nature of the processing be unfair or unlawful. Inconvenient and costly that this may be to data controllers, none can honestly say that individuals should be denied such rights, especially in relation to sensitive data such as that found in medical records.

Postscript

The Secretary of State for Health has produced draft regulations under section 60 of the Health and Social Care Act 2001. The draft regulations are the Health Services (Control of Patient Information) Regulations 2002 and extend to England and Wales only. Some concern has been expressed as to whether the draft regulations will prejudice patient confidentiality and whether they are consistent with the Data Protection Act 1988 (the views of the Patient Information Advisory Group were sought). The regulations would allow the construction and maintenance of databases by cancer registries for the purposes of monitoring the incidence of cancer, the effectiveness of treatment and screening programmes and the quality and outcomes of cancer care.

Processing will be permitted for the recognition, control and prevention of communicable diseases and other health risks such as E.coli and VCJD. The regulations also set out the circumstance in which confidential patient information may be processed for medical purposes, for example, by making identification of patients less easy and for identifying persons who may be asked to consent to use of tissue or other samples for medical purposes.

The views of the Information Commissioner on these proposals and guidance on other aspects of processing of health data can be seen in: The Information Commissioner, Use and Disclosure of Health Data, May 2002, available at the Information Commissioner's website and reproduced at Appendix 4 of this book.

PART II
THE POLICY

CHAPTER 3
MEDICAL GOVERNANCE

Dr Alan O'Rourke, Lecturer, Institute of General Practice and Primary Care, Sheffield University

Introduction: the significance of personal medical records

Data security and confidentiality are relatively new concepts in healthcare. Time was when personal medical records, if they existed at all, were probably written in Latin, and therefore not accessible to those outside a small educated class, and where the only method of dissemination was by laborious long-hand copying. Gradually, medicine evolved an arcane, shorthand of symbols, abbreviations and semi-classical terms, comprehensible to an even smaller cadre. Discretion, about what to tell relatives, colleagues, the agents of the state and even the patients themselves was another quality assumed to be an inherent part of professional etiquette. A doctor, as an educated gentleman, exercised his judgement over when to speak and when to keep his peace. Either way, he was unlikely to have to answer in court for disclosure.

Three great forces have changed this:

- Patients are better educated and more aware of their rights to see, understand and control access to their records. These rights are now backed up by complex legislation, and any professionals breaching these risk legal censure.

- The contents of medical records are far more significant for all patients, as they may affect their access to employment or financial services. When the analysis of individual genetic material becomes available, this will be an even bigger issue.

- Modern technology allows the storage, processing and dissemination of medical data on a scale undreamed of even a few decades ago. Many health services are keen to embrace the advantages of electronically held patient records.

In the UK, the basic principles of data security in healthcare are derived from a variety of statutes and reports, especially the Caldicott Report (see Appendix 2) and the Data Protection Act 1998. But, the Human Rights Act and new European legislation will add other obligations. Much of this legislation is so complex that even lawyers specialising in health issues cannot say how it will apply in practice until there have been some test cases. There are other regulations and secondary legislation which bear on data handling, such as the 1990 Computer Misuse Act, under which prosecution is possible for damaging or accessing unauthorised data; Health Service Circular 1999/053 on records management (available from the Department of Health Website at: *http://tap.ccta.gov.uk/doh/coin4.nsf/*); the Data Accreditation Process; and the Freedom of Information Act 2000. Also, although this fact is often overlooked, the UK is a signatory to Council of Europe Recommendations on the Protection of Medical Data, which sets out both the mandatory and permissive circumstances for the disclosure of such information. It is highly likely that some British and some European statutes are now incompatible.

Another player is the NHS Strategic Tracing Service (NSTS), which will hold the administrative details for all GP-registered patients in England and Wales, derived from two key sources: General Practice and the Registrar of Births and Deaths (via the Office of National Statistics). The NSTS will hold no clinical information.

The problem of handling clinical records without transgressing such a complex network of legal and governmental guidance is daunting for the most conscientious practitioner. So, in this chapter we will review key developments, starting with the framework of the Caldicott Report (and how its implementation has proceeded so far) and recent legislation affecting the disclosure of clinical records. We will then review some recommendations about using electronic format for patient records and highlight the relevant sections from the *Building the Information Core* papers (which anticipate genuine improvements of the quality of care flowing from such innovations) and discuss the role of the Information Policy Unit in ensuring the co-ordination of the whole process. This brings us to review some pragmatic advice form the General Medical Council on good practice in handling requests for disclosure of clinical records, leading to informed consent, including the issue of involving patients in managing their own records, and the merits of NHSnet. Finally, we flag information sharing between organisations as an important future development as medical and social care become more integrated.

Resource spot: current information on data security

The Caldicott Report: *http://www.doh.gov.uk/confiden/crep.htm*

The 1998 Data Protection Act: (see also Chapter 2 of this book) *http://www.hmso.gov.uk/acts/acts 1998/19980029.htm*

The 1998 Human Rights Act: (see also Chapter 1 of this book) *http://www.hmso.gov.uk/acts/acts1998/19980042.htm*

Council of Europe Recommendations on the Protection of Medical Data (sets out mandatory and permissive circumstances for disclosure) *http://www.cm.coe.int/ta/rec/1997/97r5.html*

The NHS Strategic Tracing Service: *http://www.nhsia.nhs.uk/nsts/*

Department of Health Information Policy Unit: *http://www.doh.gov.uk/ipu/*

Medical Research Council: ethics and best practice pages: *http://www.mrc.ac.uk/index/public_interest/public-ethics_and_best_practice.htm*

The Wisdom Resource Pack for Caldicott Guardians: *http://www.wisdomnet.co.uk/cald.asp* (to access this page, you will need to register with the Wisdom Centre: registration is free and on-line)

Lilley R, Lambden P, Newdick C. *Understanding the Human Rights Act: a tool kit for the Health Service* Abingdon: Radcliffe Medical Press, 2001. Includes a review of clinical practice and human rights; the Human Rights Act and NHS legislation; risk management; the European Convention on Human Rights. EMIS Professional Publishing's *Law for Doctors* provides periodic updates on Human Rights issues.

> **FIPR:** Foundation for Information Policy Research (studies the interaction between information technology and society, to identify technical developments with significant social impact, and promotes public understanding and dialogue between technologists and policy-makers in the UK and Europe): *http://www.fipr.org/*
>
> European Standardization for Health Informatics: *http://www.centc251.org/*
>
> Council of Europe. Convention for the protection of individuals with regard to the automatic processing of personal data (European treaty series No 108): *http://conventions.coe.int/Treaty/EN/cadreprincipal.htm*
>
> Patient Confidentiality and Caldicott Guardians (NHSE page on the interpretation and implementation of the Caldicott Report): *http://www.doh.gov.uk/ipu/confiden/*

The Caldicott Report

Dame Fiona Caldicott (and the name is important, see below!) had a remit to review the use of patient-identifiable information in the NHS, and her team produced their report in December 1997, in an attempt to solve deadlock between the British Medical Association and the Department of Health over access to electronic clinical records. The Caldicott Report had sixteen recommendations for handling patient identifiable data (see Appendix 2), but in practice these can be simplified to six principles, with the mnemonic "FIONA C" (we told you the name was significant):

F   Formally justify the purpose

I   Identifiable information only when absolutely necessary

O   Only the minimum required should be used

N   Need to know access

A   All must understand their responsibilities

C   Comply with and understand the law

Implementing Caldicott

Each organisation, whether acute trust, Primary Care Group (PCG) or
Primary Care Trust (PCT) or health authority, must appoint a
Caldicott Guardian, with overall responsibility for data security and
implementation of the Caldicott principles. In practice, some
organisations now have dedicated data security officers. At a practice
level, there should also be a lead for data security. Particular problems
apply to data flows between organisations, where the Guardian must
be confident about the destination and recipient of the data. This will
become significant as PCTs evolve closer links with social services.
Other important issues will be accuracy and maintenance of data; and
staff training and induction.

Guardians' duties include ensuring that:

- Uses of identifiable data are documented and justified.

- Access to such data is monitored and follows agreed procedures
  and protocols.

- Access to different levels of the record (administrative,
  demographic, clinical) is on a need to know basis.

- Situations where some safe-guards may be overridden (e.g. public
  health) are understood and documented to avoid abuse of these
  provisions.

- Protocols are in place for data sharing with other bodies.

- Confidentiality will be monitored with periodic checks and an
  annual report.

Initially, each organisation was expected to perform a security audit. In
the Trent Region of the NHS, this comprised eighteen standards,
grouped in three broad areas for each of which the organisation could
award itself a grade of 0 (usually indicating no data or no evidence of
addressing those issues); grade 1 (partial compliance with the
standard); grade 2 (full compliance with the standard). The following

table collates the returns for this audit for the 48 relevant organisations in Trent (see also *http://www.wisdomnet.co.uk/cgexsum.htm* for a fuller report on the baseline audit):

Trent Audit Results

Number of organisations reaching grade:	0	0/1	1	1/2	2
Staff and patients:					
Provision of information for patients	39	3	5		1
Confidentiality code of conduct for staff	11	8	17	3	9
Staff induction	7	3	34		4
Needs assessment for dealing with confidentiality	23	3	17	2	3
Training in confidentiality and security	20	6	14	5	3
Confidentiality requirements in staff contracts	2	1	11	3	31
Data Flows:					
Confidentiality in contact with other bodies	10	4	23	5	6
Mapping flows of patient identifiable data	34	4	7	1	2
Establishing ownership of data	30	3	14	1	
"Safe haven" for data entering or leaving the organisation	5		35	2	6
Protocols for sharing patient identifiable information with other organisations	24	7	11	3	3
Written and updated security policy	6	1	31		10

Internal Security:					
Recruitment and training of a security officer	10	3	29	3	3
Risk assessment programme in place	28	1	12		7
Documentation and investigation of security "incidents"	8	3	25	4	8
Monitoring of security effectiveness	6	5	26	3	8
Policy on password security	3	4	12	4	25
Controlled access to patient identifiable data for different employee groups	31	4	9	2	2

Assuming a maximum score of 36 (complete compliance with all standards), scores in Trent range from 4 to 25, with two thirds of the organisations between 10 and 18. However, statistical analysis of this management audit was limited by:

- Lack of consistency of staff completing the forms (possibly, they went to anyone who didn't duck when the envelope fell through the letter box).

- The subjective nature of completion, maybe accounting for those returning a 0–1 ("We have recognised the problem, but not really tackled them") or a 1–2 ("We have made progress, but not perfected it.").

In Trent, most organisations had concentrated on areas like induction, training and risk assessment, and planned to address Caldicott and the 1998 Data Protection legislation together as part of the Local Implementation Strategy. Information flows were seen as particularly problematic, and many respondents hoped for an electronic template for contracts.

On the basis of such audits, each Guardian was expected to prepare an out-turn report, leading to an improvement plan to raise compliance by at least one grade in specified categories. The Chief Executive had to sign off the annual report and improvement plan and submit them to the Regional NHS Executive (for PCGs/PCTs, to the health authority). For their part, regional NHS Executive offices were expected:

- To provide leadership for local Guardians.

- Manage Caldicott implementation, including reviewing annual improvement plans to ensure that they are realistic but challenging.

- Support local networks and training needs.

- Lead on information sharing protocols.

With the latest (April 2002) NHS reorganisation, into four Directorates of Health & Social Care and some thirty Strategic Health Authorities (SHAs), and the devolution of some traditional health authority functions to PCT level, these lines of accountability for reporting and training are no longer clear. It appears likely that SHAs will collate annual reports and submit them for analysis to the Information Policy Unit, while the Directorates take on leadership roles.

Recent legislation

But, the NHS cannot implement Caldicott *in vacuo*, but must proceed within the current legal provision for the security of personal data, such as medical records. Specifically, this means being aware of clinicians' obligations under the Data Protection, Human Rights and Health & Social Care Acts.

The Data Protection Act 1998

See, further, Chapter 2.

This Act now supersedes the 1984 Act. It expands coverage to *all* records, not just computer files, and lifts time limits – any data, however old and whatever medium it is stored on is covered. So, for instance it covers x-rays, faxes and laboratory reports. The Act introduces eight principles for data protection:

- Personal data shall not be processed unless at least one condition from Schedule 2 of the Act and for sensitive data at least one condition from Schedule 3 are satisfied.

- Personal data shall be obtained only for lawful purposes and not processed in any ways that are incompatible with those purposes.

- Personal data will be adequate (but not excessive) and relevant for those purposes.

- Personal data shall be accurate and kept up to date.

- Personal data shall not be retained for longer than is necessary.

- Personal data shall be processed in line with the rights of the data subjects.

- Organisations must take appropriate action to preserve the security and integrity of personal data.

- Personal data may not be transferred to countries outside the European Community that cannot provide adequate protection for that data.

Schedule 2 requires that data processing is based on consent, and is necessary for a contract, complying with legal obligations, in the interests of the subject, to discharge civil or judicial functions, or legitimate interest of third parties. Schedule 3 (covering most health data as "sensitive"), adds various restrictions, including one that the processing is carried out for "medical purposes" by a health professional or an other individual who "owes a duty of confidence." Medial purposes here includes public health, research and healthcare management.

For some principles there are problems in interpretation, for instance principle 5 about how long data may be retained. For someone running a clinical trial this may mean:

- Until the study is published
- For five years in case there are any late side effects
- Until someone has requested your raw data for a meta-analysis

The Human Rights Act 1998

See, further, Chapter 1.

This Act guarantees rights to privacy in home and family life including correspondence. It may be possible to over-rule some sections in the interest of public (but not individual) health issues.

The Health and Social Care Act 2001

A moving force behind the Act was the fear that many cancer registries, if still inputting details of new malignancy supplied directly from the doctors confirming the diagnosis, were operating outside the law.[1] Another stimulus was the ambiguity generated by the *Source Informatics* case[2] (see below). The pertinent clauses of the bill are sections 60 and 61 (see Appendix 1). Section 60 allows certain exemptions from the Data Protection Act, but as such does not comply with European regulations. Exemption is not easy: it requires a formal application justifying why such privileges should be granted. If the sponsors wish to extend these beyond twelve months, they must go back to the Secretary of State for Health and plead their case again. Section 61 establishes the criteria under which such exemptions can be sought. Oncologist and epidemiologists are the disciplines most likely to seek these powers.

These powers were highly controversial, with a group of healthcare professionals actively campaigning against these clauses in the Bill (see their Website at *http://www.gorjuss.com/medicalprivacy/*). The British Medical Association has also expressed disquiet about the impact on patient confidentiality in a press release. (*http://web.bma.org.uk/pressrel.nsf/webpubvwlink/SGOY–4TQKYL*) The main concerns were that these sections would limit patients' right to consent to the use of their medical records; interfere with legitimate research; and impair the ability of external bodies to monitor NHS performance, clinicians' workloads and suchlike.

Ethical objections have been also raised: patients may cease to have any control over the use of their personal health information, and that loss of patient trust will impair recruitment to clinical trials. There is also concern about granting the Health Secretary wide ranging discretionary powers to allow data matching between the NHS, police, Social Services, the Home Office and the Benefits Agency, or even to pass on clinical data for commercial ends, before establishing patient consent.[3] Some commentators claim these clauses may breach the Data Protection Act and the European Convention on Human Rights. In the

---

1. Brown P. Cancer registries fear imminent collapse *British Medical Journal* 2000 321: 849 *http://www.bmj.com/cgi/content/full/321/7265/849*
2. *R v Department of Health ex parte Source Informatics Ltd* [2000] 1 All ER 786.
3. Anderson R. Undermining data privacy in health information *British Medical Journal* 2001 322: 442–3 *http://www.bmj.com/cgi/content/full/322/7284/442*

future, as legislation becomes increasingly complex, some pieces of legislation may come to contradict others.

Patients will be given a greater voice through the Patient Information Advisory Group (PIAG), which will consider applications made under Section 60 of the Health and Social Care Act and advise the Secretary of State on the implementation of this, and the annual review of existing provisions.

Audit, research and the *Source Informatics* Case

Although some of this legislation has been pro-active, some sections have been drafted to deal with ambiguities in current data handling practices. A specific, and important case, with wide ranging implications for the traditional uses of clinical records to support processes like research and audit, was *Source Informatics* (see footnote 2 above).

Source Informatics supplied pharmaceutical companies with anonymised patient data. The court case hinged on stopping this process, but left the Department of Health in an ambivalent situation, because it found itself trying to defend the use of anonymised clinical data under certain circumstances. The final decision was that anonymised data *can* be used, as long as the process is carried out within the 1998 Data Protection Act. Some legal commentators however regard this as a fudge, as it seems to say that breaches of privacy may be justified by the circumstances.

The use of anonymised and pseudo-anonymised data for research and audit has raised much dust.[4] Purists hold that data can only be used for the purposes for which it was originally collected, unless the patient has given explicit consent. So, information collected as part of clinical care cannot be later used for an audit of the provision of that care unless the patient agrees. Also, audit clerks and researchers usually need only a small part of the record (a specific intervention, a specific outcome). They have no need to access social, marital, family or past medical details. Nor, often, do they need to identify individual patients. So, under the "need to know" principal for access to clinical records, they should not be allowed access to the whole record, but only the data they need for the audit or research project. This seems to assume that clinicians owing a "duty of care" may need to extract that data in an anonymised form. In the future, this may actually

4.   Al-Shahi R, Warlow C. Using patient-identifiable data for observational research and audit *British Medical Journal* 2000 321: 1031–1032
     http://www.bmj.com/cgi/content/full/321/7268/1031

become easier, with electronic records, password protected access to various "layers" of the record and the capacity to generate anonymised aggregates. But, while most notes continue as large files of paper, containing all sorts of sensitive data, it remains problematic.

Audit has traditionally tried to work as an educational rather than a disciplinary tool: anonymity was always an incentive to participation. But, this anonymity is not secure: lawyers may request disclosure of clinical audit records if they think these may benefit their client's case. There is no specific law relating to disclosure of audit records in the UK, so a test case will be required to establish the lawyers' rights to see such records.[5] A patient may, of course, under the Data Protection Act, ask to see any of their clinical records, including copies of x-rays, ECGs etc. There is an absolute upper limit of £50 expenses the NHS body may recoup from the patient, so this may be a further drain on public funds, as well as staff time in locating and reproducing these documents.

As a small footnote, although a patient's records (or more accurately, the media they are kept on, sheets of paper or computer files), may be the property of the Department of Health or the Health Authority, that does not confer rights of disclosure. So, if a patient "chooses" to disclose their medical details to the press about poor hospital care, even if the Trust held documentary evidence which could rebut those accusations, it could not present them to, the journalists without breaching its duty of confidentiality to the ex-patient!

Electronic Patient Records in General Practice

A key component in the modernisation of the NHS will be the application of electronic formats to store clinical data, offering solutions to the problems of accessibility, legibility and consistency of nomenclature found in traditional records. From October 2000, GPs were released from their contractual obligations to maintain such paper-based clinical records. In preparing for the wider move to electronic records, in August 2000, the British Medical Association's General Practice Committee and the Royal College of General Practitioners produced guidelines for Electronic Patient Records (EPRs) in general practice, recognising the multiple applications of patient record for clinical, research, administrative and contractual purposes, with the following recommendations (for implementation, see Chapter 5 below):

---

5.   Womack C, Roger S, Lavin, M. Disclosure of clinical audit records in law: risks and possible defences *British Medical Journal* 1997 315: 1369–1370
      http://www.bmj.com/cgi/content/full/315/7119/1369

- The practice should have an adequate supply of appropriately located work stations, with enhanced authentication mechanisms for users.

- Each practice should have electronic storage and back-up facilities, including a disaster recovery plan, to meet current and projected future growth in the volume of clinical records.

- Many practices will need the infrastructure to support a local area network (LAN), and access to a disseminated system such as NHSnet.

- All NHS systems should use a common coding system (such as a revision of the Read System) to facilitate data sharing, while recognising clinicians' continuing need for free text to record the richness of consultations.

- The record should include clinical summaries, making clear which medical problems are still active, rather than part of the past medical history, and including information from existing, but often bulky, manual GP records.

- Manual data from clinics, out of hours visits and other episodes, must be recorded and incorporated into the electronic record, until mechanisms for automatic data capture become widely used.

- Each practice must develop a security policy such that only appropriately trained personnel are entering data, with clear audit trails of who is making or amending each entry and protocols for checking the identity of any third parties requesting access to clinical information.

Issues still to settled include the retention of paper records from outside the practice and the electronic transfer of records to other practices when the patient re-registers. The full text of this document is available on-line in PDF at: *http://www.doh.gov.uk/gpepr/index.htm*

Building the Information Core (2001)

In 1998, the new government set out its medium term information strategy for the NHS. Approaching the mid-point of this programme, the government has added several new papers, reviewing progress and refining targets. One of these, *Building the Information Core* (see Appendix 3), emphasizes government determination that the effective clinical applications of IM&T will deliver very obvious improvements in the care the NHS provides to individual patients, by placing "workable and person centred systems and solutions throughout the NHS." This is in the wider context of "e-government," with wholesale innovations in harnessing new communication technologies to the delivery of public services. For the NHS, there is an evolving five year plan, encompassing:

- Completion of current programmes of connecting all GPs to NHSnet and providing all NHS staff with desk-top computer access.

- Greater provision of health information to NHS users, including NHS Direct and the use of a variety of media to reach the "information poor." The paper envisages extensive empowerment of patients in choosing appointments and referral times, including the possible use of remote tele- or video-consultations to save travelling and waiting.

- Providing healthcare professionals with reliable and convenient decision support systems, to promote best practice across the country in all clinical disciplines.

- Development of e-commerce within the NHS, and closer links with commercial IT suppliers.

- Greater standardisation of technical and managerial processes throughout the NHS.

- Adoption of the BS7799 Standards to produce a widely applied code of practice for information security.

- The incorporation of healthcare informatics into the training and education curricula of all professionals working in the NHS.

The message is certainly very up beat, and "patient centred," insisting that IM&T must deliver the sort of healthcare provision the public desire. Recent funding allocation to the NHS may relieve some of the pressures on resources, but the paper seems to gloss over more fundamental challenges, such as recruitment problems. It also makes rather sweeping assumptions that what many users want is large volumes of filtered bio-medical information, with little consideration of what they will do with the data. As with many other promises about healthcare, it has little if anything to say about patients' duty to use the system wisely: it promotes a consumerist, rather than a responsible public approach.

Building the Information Core: Protecting and Using Confidential Patient Information – a strategy for the NHS (2001)

This associated paper affirms the Government's commitment to informed consent as the basic principal underpinning the use of clinical information, while balancing rights to privacy against the public benefits of information sharing. It recognises on the one hand the rights patients have acquired, through recent legislation, and on the other the low level of awareness of confidentiality issues among NHS staff, and some recent deficiencies in obtaining consent, such as for organ retention by pathologists. The message seems to be that implied consent, although appropriate for some health transactions, has been abused, and many procedures now demand more formal and informed consent. The Information Commissioner (as the Data Protection Commissioner is now styled), has also expressed concern over the lack of transparency in the NHS over what happens to an individual's clinical data. Interim feedback from the PERIC project at the School of Health and Related Research, Sheffield University, suggests that patients initially vote for very high levels of consent and confidentiality, but that if it is explained that such processes cost the NHS time and money, and may ultimately delay their treatment, they are quite happy to accept rather less rigorous rules.[6] Again, the strategy for bringing the NHS up to scratch includes defining national standards, and educating staff, including introducing formal training in confidentiality at the nursing and medical school level. In the future, the Unique Patient Identifier number is expected to deliver pseudo-anonymisation via a tight encryption algorithm.

The Department of Health Information Policy Unit

The NHS is a huge organisation, with many component parts, such as Trusts, PCTs and SHAs exercising various degrees of local autonomy. It is essential however, that for the IM&T programme, national standards apply, both technically and managerially. So, in 1999, the Department of Health established the Information Policy Unit to provide NHS wide

6. Carlisle J. Research seminar, Sheffield May 2002

leadership in implementing the information strategy, by ensuring integrated policy between the Department of Health and the NHS Executive, including the provision of expert advice and commissioning work at national levels. It is organised into five teams:

- Cultural Change, Consumers and Communications: with educational responsibilities for both patients and staff.

- Direct Care Information: concerned with data and information standards and electronic records.

- Management Information Policy: exploring the extraction of NHS management information from operational information.

- Infrastructure Policy: developing technical standards and codes of practice.

- Implementation Review: monitoring how the various components of the NHS progress with implementing the information strategy.

Up to date details of the Unit's activities are available at: *http://www.doh.gov.uk/ipu/*

Interpreting the rules: General Medical Council Guidelines

Faced with such a complex mass of legislation, clinicians need help in interpreting them and applying to daily practice. Among the guides is *Confidentiality: protecting and providing information* (London: General Medical Council, 2000, and on their Website at: *http://www.gmc-uk.org/*). This reminds doctors that one of their professional obligations is to respect and protect confidential information, and most specifically that they should *not* disclose such information without consent. Doctors should remember that there are sins of both omission and commission: passing on data in response to improper requests, identifying patients in casual conversations or leaving faxes or computer records where they can be read by unauthorised third parties all represent breaches of this duty.

Some "information sharing," is of course an intrinsic part of delivering clinical care. For example, in a consultation, the patient will expect that the first clinician they see may need to write a referral letter to a specialist, summarising the clinical data. In fact, failure to communicate such material is more likely to provoke complaint about the frustration of having to relate clinical histories on multiple occasions. However, the clinician may need to be explicit where information may be passed on to other organisations, such as social care, where the patient may not have considered the implications of sharing sensitive data.

Disclosure without consent is the main pitfall. The onus here falls on the clinician to try all avenues to obtain informed consent. Where the patient cannot be persuaded, the practitioner must either respect that view, or make sure that they can justify disclosure on grounds that preserving privacy creates greater risks to the patient or the wider community. An example would be a patient with recently diagnosed epilepsy who refuses to surrender their driving license, where the need to protect other road users over-rides the individual right to privacy. The patient should still be told that their details are being disclosed, even if the doctor has failed to obtain their permission.

This duty includes reports to employers or insurance companies, where the applicant's consent is still needed. However, for Government bodies, written notice from an officer that the subject has given consent is acceptable. A copy of this document should be retained with the clinical notes. For research projects, where consent for access to clinical data cannot be obtained, this fact should be raised with the relevant ethics committee. "Disclosure" includes the use of records and photographs in academic journals, however limited their circulation. The doctor must of course comply with legal requirements to supply clinical data, such as for coroners' work and death certificates. But, the doctor must be wary that some requests for access to medical records may not be in line with current data protection legislation, and that such requests may include official demands: from insurance agencies, the police or the Benefits Agency.

The GMC booklet suggests a number of good practice points, which even if not carrying full legal weight, represent professional consensus for avoiding conflict:

- Keep patients informed about potential uses of their clinical data after anonymisation (such as audit and research).

- Assure yourself sure that those you are disclosing data to understand confidentiality.

- Using anonymised data wherever practical.

- Document specific patient wishes regarding their data.

- Record financial and administrative data separately from clinical material. Electronic records may actually make this easier, by having pass word protected access to various "layers:" receptionists may have access to demographic data; clinical staff access to general medical history; only the patient's regular GP may be allowed to look at sensitive episodes, such as psychiatric or sexual problems.

- Even when the patient is deceased, consider the impact of disclosure on surviving relatives.

Informed consent

.. [To medical students] *We'll open him up from here to here* [to patient] *.... don't worry, my man, this doesn't concern you at all.*
> Sir Lancelot Spratt in one of the *Doctor in the House* films.

British practice was often based on implicit consent: taking off your shirt means you agree to having your chest examined; offering your arm means you are happy to give a blood sample. But, such traditional relaxed views on consent in research and publication are now out-dated[7], as we move away from paternalism and towards "informed consent" as the standard requirement for initiating interventions. It seems unlikely that the old fashioned "operation consent form" now carries much legal authority. In research, this will cause particular problems in observational studies, or open ended interviews, where at the end the subject may reflect and withdraw consent for the use of some statements they have made.

7.   Smith R. Informed consent: edging forwards (and backwards) *British Medical Journal* 1998 316: 949–951. *http://www.bmj.com/cgi/content/full/316/7136/949*

The Houseman's tale: the consent form

A regular task for the most junior and inexperienced member of the surgical team was always "consenting the patient," quite possibly not one of your own when on the eve of their surgery, an alarmed ward sister found an unsigned form. The whole process was aptly summarised "as consenting a patient you had never met for an eponymous procedure you had never heard of."

"What's this Puti-Plat operation then, doc? How long does it take?"

"Er....[hopefully] it's something to do with your ankle...."

"But my feet are fine: it's my left shoulder. Will I need to wear a sling after?"

"Uh....just sign here like a good chap."

On close inspection the form seemed to say that a surgeon (none in particular) would perform a procedure and anything else that was found necessary at the time (I don't think it even guaranteed you any particular sort of anaesthesia). "Sorry about the big scar: had to take your colon out with the appendix and a few other odds and ends."

On one occasion I was bleeped to (and refused) to get a drowsy theatre case who had already had the pre-med to sign a consent form.

This agenda reminds us that obligations around clinical data also have a positive and pro-active side, linking with current policy on empowering patients to make informed decisions about their healthcare. Data protection is not just about denying access: modern healthcare requires doctors to provide patients with information that is appropriate in timing, volume and complexity about their illnesses and treatments, and to ensure that data is used in the patient's best interest.

Current research (e.g. the PERIC Project at Sheffield University's School of Health and Related Research) is examining the new topic of patient attitudes to their records and consent. PERIC uses a series of scenarios or vignettes, to see how different age groups and social classes feel about various professional groups (clinicians, managers, researchers) having access to various levels of their record (demographic, current medical problem, past medical history, "sensitive" episodes), for various purposes (clinical care, education, research, audit, planning). One solution is to make patients guardians of their own records, deciding who has access to various levels, and empowering them in managing their own data. A Web-based model has been proposed for this.[8]

NHSnet: a secure network?

NHSnet was originally promoted as a secure intra-net for health data. However, current advice is that records with patient identifiable data should *not* be sent over NHSnet unless encrypted, and that anyone sending such data is individually responsible for breaches of confidentiality. NHSnet will soon be upgraded to cope with increasing demand. It now includes gateways for third parties, if they have fulfilled security audits and connection codes. Social services do not yet have direct access: they may either use a Trust link with a robust firewall, or use a third party gateway. The current target for seamless encryption is early 2002, but the P-Net pilot for pathology messaging had not been commissioned as planned in December 2000, so this is likely to arrive a little late. So far, NHS net does seem fairly "hacker-proof."

Information sharing protocols

Data flows between organisations seems to be a particular problem, with the risk of patient identifiable clinical data arriving falling into the wrong hands, or being read by third parties en-route. To some extent this is not a new problem: for many years there has been concern over laboratory reports and other information faxed to GPs ending up on the desk in a reception room used by many staff. Many GPs have learned to be wary of requests for medical reports which come from bodies like the DHSS or the police. In the future, PCTs are expected to integrate with social care, generating whole new flows of data between health and social services departments. Clinical data may also need to flow to and from private health insurers and hospitals. The new NHS IT strategy envisages large volumes of clinical data, such as laboratory reports and referral letters, moving electronically between acute trusts and PCTs. Ultimately, Caldicott Guardians may find

---

8.   Schoenberg R, Safran C. Internet based repository of medical records that retains patient confidentiality *British Medical Journal* 2000 321: 1199–1203
http://www.bmj.com/cgi/content/full/321/7270/1199

themselves responsible if this data falls in to the wrong hands. NHS Executive is now developing protocols for these flows.

Resource spot: Data sharing

NHSE information sharing protocols:
http://www.doh.gov.uk/confiden/protocols.htm

Data Protection Act: guidance to Social Services:
http://www.doh.gov.uk/scg/datap.htm

Association of Directors of Social Services, Information Management Group (especially the Information sharing with the NHS Group: scroll down the page for this link):
http://www.ssimg.freeserve.co.uk/Work_programme/index.htm

Kohane I, van Wingerde F, Fackler J, Cimino C, Kilbridge P, Murphy S. Sharing electronic medical records across multiple heterogeneous and competing institutions. *Proceedings of the American Medical Institute Association Annual Fall Symposium* 1996:608–12.

Summary

- Traditionally, the confidentiality of medical records was guaranteed by the format they were recorded in.

- Recent legal and technical developments have raised the profile of medical data, which may be highly significant to the individual for employment and financial services.

- The Caldicott Report and recent legislation provide a framework for the legal handling of clinical data.

- However the legislation is complex, may be contradictory and may not fit in with European laws.

- In practice, test cases and future research, including patient attitudes to the use of their data and consent, will inform data handling in the NHS.

- Each NHS organisation is required to appoint a Caldicott Guardian to oversee data security work, and perform a base line audit of current compliance with standards in this area.

- It seems prudent for clinicians to handle data within the rules of the 1998 Data Protection Act, and if there are doubts or problems to refer to their Caldicott Guardian.

- The basic rule is that the patient should know of and approve any uses their clinical data is put to. Where the patient declines such consent, the doctor must have good and well documented grounds for disclosure.

Topics for debate:

What sorts of detail make a piece of clinical information "patient identifiable"? How can records be processed to produce "anonymised" or "pseudo-anonymised data"?

Which bits of your own medical records would you feel happy about others having access to? Which sections should administrative staff, clinical staff, managerial staff or researchers have access to? Would you like to be able to impose restrictions on the use your data is put to?

What do you think constitute "sensitive" episodes, which require anonymisation or higher levels of security?

What are the strengths and weaknesses of allowing patients to administer their own records?

Which organisations does your organisation share sensitive data with?

If you were on a group charged with developing an information sharing protocol, which key areas would you need to cover?

How would your organisation score in an audit of data security and handling? For areas of weakness, what *could* be done to improve compliance and what is being done? It may be worth talking to your Caldicott Guardian, IT department or data security officer. You might jog their minds over some little jobs on the list!

Suggestions for further reading

Bergeron B. How to safeguard your clinical data. Security systems against crashes, thieves, and hackers. *Postgraduate Medicine* 1999 105(1):27–9

Denley I, Smith S, Gardner M, O'Conor R. Privacy in clinical information systems in secondary care *British Medical Journal* 1999 318: 1328–1331.
http://www.bmj.com/cgi/content/full/318/7194/1328

Department of Health *Building the Information Core – implementing the NHS Plan* London: Dept of Health 2001 and at:
http://www.doh.gov.uk/ipu/strategy/overview/index.htm

Department of Health Information Policy Unit *Building the Information Core: Protecting and Using Confidential Patient Information – a strategy for the NHS* Dept of Health: London 2001 and at:
http://www.doh.gov.uk/ipu/confiden/

Epstein M, Pasieka M, Lord W, Wong S, Mankovich N. Security for the digital information age of medicine: issues, applications, and implementation. *Journal of Digital Imaging* 1998 11: 1, 33–44.

Etchells E, Sharpe G, Walsh P, Williams J, Singer P. Bioethics for clinicians: 1. Consent. *Canadian Medical Association Journal* 1996 155:177–80.

Gostin L. Health care information and the protection of personal privacy: ethical and legal considerations. *Annals of Internal Medicine* 1997 127: 683–690

Hewson B. Why the Human Rights Act matters to doctors *British Medical Journal* 2000 321: 780–781.
http://www.bmj.com/cgi/content/full/321/7264/780

Hodge J, Gostin L, Jacobson P. Legal issues concerning electronic health information: privacy, quality, and liability *Journal of the American Medical Association* 1999 282: 1466–1471

Houghton G. PCGs, Caldicott and Confidentiality *Journal of Clinical Governance* 2000 8: 3–4.

Kelly G. Patient data, confidentiality, and electronics *British Medical Journal* 1998 316:718–719
http://www.bmj.com/cgi/content/full/316/7133/718

Lee-Winser J. Security. The Data Protection Act: a decade of data protection in the NHS. *British Journal of Healthcare Computing & Information Management*. 1995 12(5):20–1.

Mandl K, Szolovits P, Kohane I, Markwell D, MacDonald R. Public standards and patients' control: how to keep electronic medical records accessible but private *British Medical Journal* 2001 322: 283–7: *http://www.bmj.com/cgi/content/full/322/7281/283*

Medical Defence Union *Confidentiality*. London: MDU, 2001 (Concise booklet discussing the legal aspects of disclosure of clinical data, with specific references to sexual and reproductive health, children, the mentally ill and the deceased.)

Medical Defence Union *Can I see the records*? London: MDU, 2001 (Concise booklet discussing good practice in clinical record keeping, legal obligations under the Human Rights and Data Protection Acts and disclosure during court hearings.)

Smith E, Eloff J. Security in health-care information systems – current trends. *International Journal of Medical Informatics*. 1999 54(1):39–54.

Strobl J, Cave E, Walley T. Data protection legislation: interpretation and barriers to research *British Medical Journal* 2000 321: 890–892. *http://www.bmj.com/cgi/content/full/321/7265/890*

Walker P. Caldicott implementation: protecting and using confidential patient information in the modern NHS. *British Journal of Healthcare Computing & Information Management* 1998 15(7):28–30.

Wells, M. Caldicott guardians and the NHS Strategic Tracing Service *British Journal of Healthcare Computing & Information Management*. 1998 15(7):32–5.

PART III
THE PRACTICE

CHAPTER 4
CONFIDENTIALITY: SIMPLE RISK-MANAGEMENT MEASURES

Sandy Anthony, The Medical Protection Society

Information about patients is being shared and transmitted daily within and between healthcare organisations and, to a lesser extent, between different agencies and some commercial interests such as insurance companies. The magnitude of this information flow is such that patient confidentiality is probably being breached inadvertently on a daily basis.

Most of these breaches are likely to go unnoticed by patients but this does not exonerate healthcare workers from their obligation to treat all personal information about their patients with the utmost care. They not only have professional and contractual duties to protect the confidentiality of their patients, but this principle is also enshrined in common law and, more recently, has been formally set out in legislation.

There is now a plethora of legislation governing the use of patient information – the Data Protection Act 1998, the Computer Misuse Act 1990 and the Human Rights Act 1998 being the main ones. Although the legislation is complex and difficult to fathom, its spirit is clear:

- personal information and sensitive personal information should not be held or used without good reason and without the individual's knowledge and consent;

- such information must be kept securely and not be imparted to others without the individual's consent;

- the person the information relates to has the right to see and check the content.

This means that besides protecting patient information you have a duty to let your patients know what sort of uses may be made of their personal information and the categories of people who may be accessing it. Patients also need to be made aware of their right to withhold consent to disclosure and their right of access to their records.

The overriding principle that governs the use and sharing of information is that it should be in the patient's best interests and in accordance with his/her wishes. The only exceptions to this are when the safety of others is being compromised or when the information is being used for the greater public good – e.g. epidemiological research, cancer registries, etc.

In the rare instance that the former situation arises – e.g. a mentally disturbed patient has confided his intention of killing someone, a patient with AIDS refuses to tell her sexual partner about her condition, a patient with epilepsy is continuing to drive, you suspect that a child is being sexually abused – your best course of action is to telephone your defence organisation and talk the matter over with a medico-legal adviser. If you do decide that a breach of confidence is justified in the circumstances, you should inform the patient of your intentions if this is at all feasible and you should scrupulously document what you have done and your reasons for doing it.

Although it is becoming increasingly common to use GP patient records for research purposes, this activity is not yet covered by specific legislation; it is likely, however, that its legality will soon be clarified by future statutory instruments.

Identifying the risks

From a risk-management perspective, there are four spheres of activity that could benefit from a risk assessment. They are:

- Environment
- Practice policy/protocols/work practices
- Access and information flows
- Keeping patients informed

Environment

It goes without saying that sensitive personal information like medical records should be kept securely to prevent access by unauthorised people. This can be interpreted very differently from organisation to organisation, though. Some think that as long as the premises are secured out of hours they are safe from unwarranted intrusion. These are trusting souls who cannot imagine that their patients or visiting tradesmen and outside contractors would be nosy enough to look at other people's records. We have seen surgeries where the medical records are stored in the waiting room, fax machines in public-access corridors, bundles of Lloyd George records left lying on desks and reception counters and so on. This sort of set-up is just tempting fate and can do nothing to reassure patients that their own information is being treated in confidence.

When assessing how your own environment shapes up as a repository of confidential information, ask yourself the following questions:

- Are the medical records stored in a lockable room accessible only to authorised personnel?

- Are computer monitors positioned in such a way that they can't be overlooked?

- Are printers and fax machines located in secure areas?

- Do you have special wastebins (or shredders) for the secure disposal of personal information? How often are they emptied (and by whom)? Where are they located?

- Are consultation rooms soundproof?

- Are there areas in which staff discussing patient care may be overheard?

- Do rooms with computer terminals have locks on the doors?

- Is the appointment book kept where it cannot be easily seen by patients?

- Is seating in the waiting room placed at a distance from the reception desk?

- Does the layout of the reception area discourage patients from queuing up at the desk?

- Do receptionists have access to a telephone out of hearing of waiting patients?

- Can the reception office be closed off from the waiting room if necessary (e.g. when only one person is on duty and she has to leave the room)?

Although purpose-built surgeries do exist, the vast majority of GP practices are based in converted premises. The success of these conversions is variable, but practices do seem to share a widespread problem with the layout of their reception and waiting rooms. Even in purpose-built surgeries it can be difficult to avoid inadvertent breaches of confidentiality. Many have been designed as open-plan spaces to convey a sense of accessibility, but there is an inevitable trade-off between openness and privacy that, in the end, has to be mediated by the staff. Even so, there are measures that you could consider taking (within your budgetary constraints) to modify the environment. Examples are:

- Playing background music in the waiting room.

- Installing thicker doors on consultation rooms.

- Allocating an area where patients can speak in confidence to the receptionist if they need to.

- Installing a glass screen across the reception desk. This has the added benefit of enhancing staff security.

- Adjusting the height or width of the reception desk – if it is too wide, patients may have to raise their voices to be heard and if it is too low, papers can be too easily seen.

- If it is not possible to move a computer out of the range of sight of visitors, consider investing in flat screens that can only be viewed from the front.

Practice policies/protocols/work practices

Practice policy

Every practice should have a clearly stated confidentiality policy and all staff contracts should include a confidentiality clause (see chapter 5 page 109 for an example clause). It is worth reviewing your confidentiality policy to see whether it could benefit from being more explicit. You could, for example, set out a policy that includes:

- An explanation of why it is so important to preserve patients' confidentiality – the ethical and legal imperatives.

- What confidentiality means in practice – e.g. accessing information only on a 'need to know' basis in the patient's interests, not out of curiosity or for any other reason; not releasing information to third parties without the patient's consent; not discussing patients in public places; not divulging patients' addresses or phone numbers to unauthorised people; logging off before leaving a computer unattended; keeping papers containing personal information out of the sight and reach of unauthorised people.

- Who the policy covers – i.e. staff, clinicians, students, volunteers and any other person associated with patient care.

- The kind of information governed by the principle – i.e. names and addresses, information in and about medical records, test results, appointments, prescriptions and referrals.

- Disciplinary measures that may be applied in the event of a breach of confidentiality.

Protocols

The confidentiality document should be supported by a series of protocols covering areas such as the following:

- Seeking a patient's consent before releasing information. (See GMC guidance.)

- Disclosing patient information to outside agencies (e.g. social services, the police).

- Disclosing patient information to interested third parties (e.g. relatives, insurance companies).

- Disclosing information about patients who have died.

- Using patient information for research and audit.

- Keeping access to information on a 'need to know' basis. (See Caldicott Guardian's manual.[1])

- Storing and accessing highly sensitive patient information (e.g. HIV status). (See *www.doh.gov.uk/nhsexipu/confiden/gpcd/index* for a sample form and security wrapper for the notes.)

- Obtaining patients' consent to disclosure.

- Receiving and transmitting patient-identifiable information. (See Caldicott Guardian's manual.[1])

- Checking the identity of callers before giving out information – e.g. test results. Accepted practice is to ask the caller for his/her date of birth and address. Some practices also ask the caller to confirm the date on which the test was taken. Another idea is to issue the patient with a unique password.

- Checking that you have the right set of notes by confirming a patient's date of birth before giving them access to their records.

- If records are held electronically, procedures for creating and safely storing back-up disks. (See *Good Practice Guidelines for General Practice Electronic Patient Records.*[2])

Some of the above can be incorporated into patient information leaflets and notices and all of it could usefully be reproduced in your staff handbook, if you have one.

Training

Patient confidentiality should be an integral part of staff induction, but should also be re-visited with regular training sessions. Your Caldicott Guardian should be able to help with this.

---

1. Department of Health *Protecting and Using Patient Information: A Manual for Caldicott Guardians*, 1999, Leeds: NHS Executive.
2. Joint Computing Group of the General Practitioners' Committee and the Royal College of General Practitioners (2000) *Good Practice Guidelines for General Practice Electronic Patient Records,* Leeds: NHS Executive.

Access and information flows

The fourth Caldicott principle states that 'Access [to patient-identifiable information] should be on strict need-to-know basis'.[3] The level of access granted to each member of the practice must be justifiable, given the tasks and functions that the individual needs to carry out and in the context of the patient's best interests. If you hold all your records electronically and your software complies with the specifications for RFA99,[4] it should be relatively straightforward to restrict certain types of information to different users.

Although the Caldicott guidelines acknowledge that it is easier to restrict access with electronic records, the principle also extends to manual files: for example, 'staff who need access to manual files for filing purposes should not need to access the information already contained within the files'[3] p.2). Obviously, one depends much more on the staff member's sense of honour in these circumstances. If the practice has a strongly reinforced ethos of respecting patient confidentiality backed up by regular reviews of staff training needs, compliance should not be a problem.

Sharing information with other organisations

Reasons for sharing confidential patient information between two organisations fall into two categories:

1. Care and treatment of the patient.
2. Any purpose other than patient care.

Unless the patient has specifically requested otherwise, and as long as he/she has been told that personal information may be shared in this way, you do not need to obtain express consent to pass on personal information, in confidence, to others engaged in providing care and treatment.

---

3. Department of Health *Protecting and Using Patient Information: A Manual for Caldicott Guardians*, 1999, Leeds: NHS Executive.
4. NHS Information Authority *Primary Care Computer Systems – Requirements for Accreditation*, 2001 RFA99 V1.2.

If you are sharing information for any other reason (e.g. epidemiological research, education, clinical audit, administration), the GMC[5] offers the following guidance:

a. seek patients' consent to disclosure of any information wherever possible, whether or not you judge that patients can be identified from the disclosure.

b. Anonymise data where unidentifiable data will serve the purpose.

c. Keep disclosures to the minimum necessary.

Note: for the time being, the GMC,[4] 4.11 has made an exception to this rule with regard to providing information for cancer registries.

Sharing information with third parties

The questions relating to confidentiality that we get asked most about at MPS concern disclosure to third parties such as relatives, solicitors, insurance companies, employers or the police. Although each incident may have its own unique attributes, it is still worthwhile arming yourself with a set of protocols or guidelines that covers the scenarios you and your staff are most likely to encounter.

You could, for example, work out with receptionists an appropriate script that they can adopt when they are asked particular questions on the telephone – relatives enquiring about a patient's appointment or test results, police wanting the address of a patient, employers checking that a patient attended the surgery on a certain day, and so on.

In all but the most exceptional circumstances the rule is that personal information about a patient should never be disclosed to a third party without the patient's consent. The exceptions that might apply are when the patient is not capable of giving or withholding consent (in which case you should decide whether disclosure is in his or her best interests) or when disclosure could prevent serious harm befalling another person.

It is not possible (or even advisable) to devise protocols or guidelines to cover every possible eventuality and you will still be faced with tricky problems for which you will need to seek advice from a colleague or your defence organisation. Domestic disputes in which parents are

---

4. NHS Information Authority *Primary Care Computer Systems – Requirements for Accreditation,* 2001 RFA99 V1.2.
5. General Medical Council *Confidentiality: Protecting and Providing Information,* 2000, London.

fighting over access to their children's records is a common problem, for example, to which there is generally no easy formulaic response. Requests for disclosure from solicitors, on the other hand, are generally more straightforward: if the solicitor is acting for the patient concerned, or has acquired the patient's consent, then you should comply with the request.

Keeping patients informed

Medical records have evolved over the years into much more than the simple doctor's *aide-mémoire* that they started out as. Nowadays a patient's record plays a crucial role in continuity of care delivered by a multiplicity of healthcare professionals; in the event of legal proceedings relating to patient care, it is an important source of evidence that can make or break the defence of a court case; if a doctor's conduct or competence is called into question, his or her patients' records can be scrutinised keenly by disciplinary panels and other such bodies.

The contents of patients' records are also now increasingly viewed as a valuable resource that can be used to inform healthcare planning and financial audit, epidemiological research, education and so on. Just in the course of NHS administration, more people than ever before have access to patients' records and put them to uses that most patients are probably unaware of.

As keepers of these repositories of information, GP practices have a duty to tell their patients how information about them is likely to be used and what their rights are under the Data Protection Act 1998.

You can do this by notifying new patients when they register with the practice and by putting leaflets and notices in the waiting room and enclosing information sheets with letters to patients or prescriptions. These measures may not be sufficient in certain circumstance; not all patients are literate, for example, or they may be visually impaired. This is why the Department of Health,[6] 3.3, recommends 'routinely providing patients with necessary information as a part of care planning' (Department of Health 2001: 3.3).

Your Caldicott Guardian will be able to tell you what core information should be included in your notices and leaflets.[7] If you

---

6. Department of Health *The Protection and Use of Patient Information: Guidance from the Department of Health*, 2001, London.
7. See also NHS Information Authority *Between You and Me: Protecting Personal Information*, 2001 (Caldicott Toolkit containing staff training video and an 'off-line' website on CD).

want to take the drudgery out of writing your own, there are some good downloadable samples on the DoH's confidentiality website – *www.doh.gov.uk/nhsexipu/confid/gpcd/index.htm.*

Immediate action

Clinical risk management is a practical undertaking that does not lend itself easily to attempts to pin it down on paper. Each workplace has its own combination of environmental factors, resources and socio-political forces that manifest in different ways. The distribution and significance of risks varies from one organisation to another and it follows that effective risk-management solutions from one workplace do not necessarily translate well to another.

The best course of action when starting any risk-management programme, therefore, is to initiate it with a brainstorming session. Try to include as many involved members of staff as possible and encourage them to contribute fully. Everyone has their own perspective on how well existing procedures work and how they might be improved. There is an added benefit to this approach: if all staff are involved in planning changes to the surgery's work practices, they are far more likely to get behind the project to ensure its success.

Confidentiality in practice

The following are examples of some of the most common confidentiality issues doctors may encounter. They are intended to provide general guidance only. Please contact your medical protection organisation for assistance with any specific queries you may have.

Scenario 1

A patient of Dr H has been accused of assaulting his (the patient's) partner. Dr H has been asked by the patient's solicitor to confirm to the police that a conversation regarding the patient's partner took place on a particular day.

Opinion

Whether Dr H could provide this confirmation would depend on who participated in the conversation about the patient's partner. If the conversation about the patient's partner took place between this patient and Dr H, then Dr H would be at liberty to provide the requested confirmation. However, if the patient himself did not participate in this conversation, then both the subject matter of the conversation, and the fact that it took place, should remain confidential, and should not be disclosed without the express consent of the patient's partner.

Scenario 2

The custody of a child is in dispute between the two parents. Custody resides with the child's mother. All three are patients of Dr T. The father's solicitor has contacted Dr T to request the child's medical notes.

Opinion

The situation regarding this child needs to be clarified before Dr T can make a decision whether to agree to this request for disclosure. The Data Protection Act 1998 permits the disclosure of information about a child, in response to a data subject access request, to a person who has parental responsibility for that child. Under the Children Act 1989 this would be either parent, providing that they were married at the time of the child's birth. As any person with parental responsibility can act independently of the other, this would give a father with parental responsibility the right to make a subject access request relating to his child without the consent of the other parent, irrespective of who has custody. He may do this directly, or through his solicitor. However, if the child's parents were not married at the time of the child's birth, the father may not have parental responsibility. He can only acquire parental responsibility either by order of a court, or through a parental responsibility agreement with the child's mother. If he does not have parental responsibility then the records should not be disclosed without the consent of the mother, or by order of the court. The other factor to be considered is the mental capacity of this child. Under the Data Protection legislation, information can be withheld in relation to a subject access request if the child either provided the information in the expectation that it would not be disclosed to the person making the request, or if the child has requested that the information should not be disclosed. A decision to withhold information on one of these grounds would depend on the mental capacity of the child.

Scenario 3

A patient of Dr A has admitted abusing his stepdaughter twenty years ago. He now wishes to undergo counselling, although the stepdaughter does not want action to be taken. Should the patient be reported?

Opinion

Reporting the patient, e.g. to the police, will necessarily have personal consequences for the stepdaughter, and her wishes need to be taken into account. Dr A is not obliged to report the stepfather to the police purely on the basis of this admission. However, he could choose to do so as the GMC advises that disclosures may be made without consent if they may assist in the prevention, detection or prosecution of a serious crime, such as child abuse. Alternatively, Dr A could choose to respect the stepdaughter's wishes unless he believes that her stepfather currently poses a risk to children. The GMC guidance[8] states that disclosure of information without consent may be justified where a failure to do so will put either the patient or others to risk of death or serious harm and that concerns about the possible abuse of a child should be reported promptly to an appropriate responsible person or statutory agency. Dr A therefore needs to weigh several factors in the balance when deciding what to do. Firstly, whether his patient currently poses a risk to children, secondly that the police are unlikely to be able to bring a prosecution without the active co-operation of the stepdaughter, and lastly the impact on both his patient and the stepdaughter. There is a possibility that disclosure would prevent the stepfather participating in counselling, and would cause considerable distress to the stepdaughter. When making his decision Dr A must give priority to the level of risk that his patient currently poses to children. He might like to take advice about this from a consultant specialising in this area.

Scenario 4

The police have contacted Dr L to request information about a patient who has been involved in a road traffic accident. The patient had previously expressed his concern that he was being 'picked on' by the police. Is Dr L justified in withholding this information?

---

8. General Medical Council, *Confidentiality: Protecting and Providing Information*, 2000, London: GMC, sec. 4, para. 36.

Opinion

Under the Road Traffic Act 1988, Dr L has an obligation to provide the police with any information in his possession that might identify a person who is alleged to have committed an offence under the Act. Dr L therefore needs to ask the police to confirm if such an allegation is being made. If so, then he would not be justified in withholding this information even though he might wish to be sensitive to his patient's concerns. This would mean disclosing his patient's personal details, but clinical information should be withheld.

Scenario 5

Dr V's patient, now deceased, was diagnosed with Hepatitis C. Dr V now wishes to disclose this information to the deceased patient's partner, but is unsure whether GMC guidelines endorse this.

Opinion

The basic principle is that doctors still have an obligation to keep personal information confidential after the patient has died. However, disclosures can be made in some circumstances, providing they can be justified. The GMC's guidance on "Serious Communicable Diseases"[9] permits disclosure of information in order to protect another person from risk of death or serious disease providing that they are, or have been, at risk of infection. It is likely that Dr V would be able to justify providing this information to the deceased patient's partner, as it would enable him or her to be tested for Hepatitis C, and to receive appropriate advice and treatment if tests prove to be positive.

Scenario 6

One of Dr F's patients has been discovered stealing a methadone prescription. Dr F believes he should contact the police, but is now uncertain because his patient has recently found employment. Can he use his discretion in this case?

Opinion

The GMC advises[10] that disclosures may be made without consent if they may assist in the prevention, detection or prosecution of a serious crime, and in this context serious crime is defined as that

---

9. General Medical Council, *Serious Communicable Diseases*, 1997, London: GMC, para 22.
10. General Medical Council, *Confidentiality: Protecting and Providing Information*, 2000, London: GMC, sec. 4, para. 37c.

which would put someone at risk of death or serious harm, and would usually be crimes against the person. Dr F is not legally obliged to report this patient to the police even though a crime has been committed. He can therefore use his discretion in this case.

Scenario 7

Every evening, a patient of Dr G drinks alcohol excessively. He drives a school bus in the mornings. Dr G has advised the patient that he will be over the drink-drive limit, but he refuses to acknowledge this.

Opinion

The GMC advises[11] that a doctor *should* disclose information to a Medical Advisor at the DVLA if he thinks that that the patient may be a danger to himself or to others when driving, and the patient cannot be persuaded either to stop driving or to report himself to the DVLA. In the "At a Glance Guide to the Current Medical Standards of Fitness to Drive"[12] the DVLA defines Alcohol Misuse as "a state which because of consumption of alcohol, causes disturbance of behaviour, related disease or other consequences, likely to cause the patient, his/her family or society harm now, or in the future, and which may or may not be associated with dependency". Confirmation of persistent alcohol misuse will result in revocation of the holder's licence.

According to the GMC's booklet on "Confidentiality: Protecting and Providing Information"[13] it is the legal responsibility of the DVLA to decide if a person is medically unfit to drive. It states that the DVLA has to be informed when driving licence holders have a condition which affect their safety as a driver.

Firstly, you should make sure that your patient understands that his condition may impair his ability to drive. Should he be incapable of understanding this advice, for example because of dementia, you should inform the DVLA without delay. Explain to the patient that he has a legal duty to inform the DVLA about the condition. If he refuses to accept the diagnosis or the effect of the condition on his ability to drive, you can suggest that he seeks a second opinion, and make appropriate arrangements for this. You should advise him not to drive until the second opinion has been obtained. Every reasonable effort should be made to persuade the patient to stop driving when he is not

---

11.   General Medical Council, *Confidentiality: Protecting and Providing Information*, 2000, London: GMC, sec 4, para. 37b.
12.   DVLA Medical Advisory Branch, *At a Glance Guide to the Current Medical Standard of Fitness to Drive: For Medical Practitioners*, 1999, Swansea: DVLA.
13.   General Medical Council, *Confidentiality: Protecting and Providing Information*, 2000, London: GMC, appendix 2.

fit to do so. You might consider telling his next of kin, for instance. If you do not succeed in persuading him to stop driving, or you are given (or find) evidence that he is continuing to drive despite this advice, you should disclose relevant medical information immediately, in confidence, to a Medical Adviser at the DVLA. Before giving information to the DVLA you should try to inform the patient of your decision to do so. Once the DVLA has been informed, you should also write to the patient, to confirm that a disclosure has been made.

Scenario 8

A 14 year old patient has agreed to Dr R's request that he should undergo treatment for drug and alcohol problems. However, he does not want his parents to know. Is Dr R justified in withholding this information?

Opinion

Dr R may be justified in withholding this information if the 14 year old is competent, and if this course of action would be in his or her best interests. Competent young people under the age of 16 have the same basic rights to confidentiality as adults. To be 'competent' a young person would need to have sufficient intelligence and maturity to understand the nature, purpose and consequences of the treatment, including alternatives, and the consequences of non-treatment. If this patient is competent Dr R should seek to persuade the patient to involve a parent or guardian, but a refusal to do so should be respected unless it runs contrary to his or her interests. In this case Dr R may have a difficult balancing act between maintaining his patient's confidence and co-operation, and safeguarding his or her welfare. The patient's natural fears about telling his parents may prove to be unfounded and their support is likely to be valuable. Dr R would be advised to consult the Department of Health guidance "Drug Misuse and Dependence – Guidelines on Clinical Management" (1999, London, The Stationery Office and www.doh.gov.uk/drugdep.htm). This states that family involvement should be seen as good practice and that support be sought from someone with parental responsibility for any proposed treatment, as this will increase the likelihood of treatment being effective. If Dr R decides that his patient is not competent, and that withholding information will not serve the patient's interests, then he should take steps to inform a parent or guardian. He should tell the patient before doing so.

Scenario 9

The family of an Alzheimer's patient registered with Dr S have requested access to medical records. Dr S considers the patient is not competent to give consent. Is it reasonable to allow access?

Opinion

All patients, including those who lack capacity, have a right to expect that their confidentiality will be respected. Under the Data Protection Act 1998 information can be withheld in response to a data subject access request if the patient either provided the information in the expectation that it would not be disclosed to the person making the request, or if they have previously requested that the information should not be so disclosed. In considering what to do, Dr S needs to consider whether either of these circumstances applies. In relation to the GMC's guidance on confidentiality,[14] he would also need to assess whether it is essential, in the medical interests of the patient to permit access to her medical records. In order to do this he may need to ascertain why the family are making this request. It may well be reasonable for Dr S to allow access, providing that it serves the interests of the patient.

Scenario 10

During a consultation, a potentially psychopathic patient of Dr B threatens to harm his daughter's boyfriend. Should Dr B report this to either the police or social services?

Opinion

The GMC guidance[15] states that disclosure of information without consent may be justified where a failure to do so will put either the patient or others to risk of death or serious harm. It also states that disclosures may be made without consent if they may assist in the prevention, detection or prosecution of a serious crime. In this context serious crime will usually be crimes against the person. If Dr B has reasonable grounds to believe that the patient will carry out his threat and that the above circumstances apply, then he should disclose information to an appropriate person or authority. Under these circumstances this may include the police. He may wish to consider arranging for the patient to be assessed by a psychiatrist first

---

14.   General Medical Council, *Confidentiality: Protecting and Providing Information*, 2000, London: GMC, sec. 4, para. 38.

15.   Ibid, sec. 4, para. 36.

in order to obtain a second opinion on the risk that the patient poses to the boyfriend or anyone else.

Acknowledgement

Thanks are due to medico-legal adviser, Gill Talbot, for kindly providing the opinions accompanying the case scenarios.

Useful websites

Department of Health's confidentiality site
www.doh.gov.uk/ipu/confiden/

NHS Information Authority's Caldicott site
www.nhsia.nhs.uk/caldicott/

General Medical Council
www.gmc-uk.org/

NHS Scotland's dataprotection site
www.show.scot.nhs.uk/dataprotection

Information Commissioner
www.dataprotection.gov.uk

NHS Northern Ireland's confidentiality site
www.n-i.nhs.uk/dataprotect/data_protect.htm

CHAPTER 5
IT RESPONSES TO CONFIDENTIALITY ISSUES

Sean Riddell (Deputy Managing Director EMIS) and Chris Spencer (Solicitor and Product Development Director, EMIS Legal)

Introduction

Other parts of this book have dwelt on the legal and ethical issues concerning patient confidentiality – especially those that have been created or amplified by information technology.

In contrast this section – whilst containing warnings and questions – is intended to provide at least some safety measures and answers, principally through the use of information technology to promote information security.

Information security seeks to provide not only confidentiality but also integrity and availability of data. Whilst, for obvious reasons, this chapter will focus on confidentiality we think it only right to mention the other two aspects:

- integrity – information is suitable for its purpose and has not been corrupted or changed without authority;

- availability – information can be accessed and amended by those entitled whenever needed.

Information security may be compromised in many ways, accidental or deliberate, by people or things inside or outside the organisation. Despite the popular notion of the malicious hacker it is much more likely that security will be affected by accidents – either by fire, flood or some other physical damage – or by what may be known as "pilot error" within the organisation – inactivity, ineptitude and incorrect configuration.

The response to these threats may be physical or logical:

– Physical security measures will protect the system and its environment from damage or removal for example by enclosing the server in a locked, fire resistant, air cooled room with a fitted intruder alarm.

– Logical, in contrast, protection tries to protect the data from unauthorised use, for example by the use of passwords.

In the main this chapter concentrates on logical security, rather than physical and, in particular, the role that information technology itself can play here. However, we have referred to some physical aspects and the use of procedures and included a further reading section to give access to additional information on the physical aspects of information security.

We hope that the information given in this chapter helps in all three areas of risk (confidentiality, integrity and availability) but of course no security can ever be complete.

The completely secure system would not only be almost, if not entirely, unusable, but also subject to the relentless tread of time. With the benefits that come with 'new and improved', also it is followed by "new and improved" ways of compromising security.

So, our object here is to help the reader manage the risk of information insecurity and, in the case of (necessary) compromise, to improve the prospects of data recovery.

We do this in the following ways. First by an alphabetically arranged series of shorter sections concentrating on particular areas of concern. Then a longer section looking at the recommendations of the Caldicott Report.[1] Finally, some suggestions as to E-mail and Internet Policies and further reading.

---

1.   Caldicott Report (The Caldicott Committee Report on the Review of Patient – Identifiable Information, December 1997, NHS Executive, London. *See Appendix 3.*

Access Logs

The Problem

Successful unauthorised entry may well be preceded by unsuccessful attempts. Tracking those attempts may mean that authorised system users are both forewarned and forearmed.

Some Suggestions

So, it is preferable (at the very least) if the computer system keeps a record of every attempt made to use it. This should apply whether the use is successful or unsuccessful.

This record should be viewed every day and any suspicious activity investigated immediately.

Backup and verification

The Problem

At the root of all information security is a back up of the data.

This is because errors will occur: data will be lost or corrupted and so a retrievable, valid copy will be the only option.

Our certainty in making this predication is because of the wide range of threats to data. Viruses, theft of laptops or desktop machines, crashed hard disks, corruption during an update or a 'finger jerk' (as opposed to knee jerk) reaction to the seemingly endless 'Are you sure?' questions in a program installation – all can lead to catastrophic data loss. Irrecoverable except from a back up.

Backups should be taken both regularly and frequently: the relevant media stored off site after having been checked for errors. This last is crucial because of another item we could have added to our list of threats to data – backup data not saved, overwritten or corrupted during the backup process itself.

Backup software – whilst often robust and useful – is itself prone to error. Perhaps the tape was full or dirty, perhaps the relevant files to be backed up have been moved or added to, perhaps those responsible for backups forgot to press the start button, select the right files for backup or even to insert a tape.

All these things have happened and will happen again.

Some Suggestions

So, we would recommend tape verification procedures – if necessary by third parties – to ensure that what is backed up is the right data, all of the right data, in the right format, not corrupted and capable of being restored.

A well known computing organisation publicised that it verifies data sent to it in backup files before storing it for safekeeping.

Nonetheless, materials delivered have included:

- corrupt files,

- encrypted files with no decryption software,

- four floppy disks glued to a piece of wood, and

- a set of supposed back up data that turned out to be a game called 'Zelda the Leather Maiden of Phobos'.

Even if you feel tape verification is excessive, at the very least we would urge:

- daily (usually overnight) backups and extra backups before any major software installation or upgrade;

- a cycle of backups over – say – four weeks to minimise the effect if corrupt data overwrites valid data over a period;

- checking of the backup report and the taking of any necessary action;

- offsite – but easily retrievable – storage of media;

- maintenance of an offsite – but easily retrievable – cache of the installation files for the operating and applications (and backup) programs used on the system – data alone is useless without its infrastructure and a means of retrieving it;

- data media and the cache of installation files should be kept in a locked fireproof media safe;

- frequent renewal of backup media due to tape wear and general degradation;

- purging or (safer) archiving of redundant data so minimising data storage requirements for current data.

Data Destruction

The Problem

Whilst in most cases data retention is the objective of an information security policy, sometimes data destruction is required.

Otherwise, for example, a replaced faulty hard drive may find its way to unauthorised users.

That drive may contain unerased data and, even if data has been erased, the data may still be recovered by the more technically aware unauthorised user. This is because 'erasing' data in effect simply deletes the links between the table of contents held by the system in relation to the drive rather than the actual data to which those links refer. So, unless the data is overwritten by other data, it may be recovered quite easily.

Even normal formatting of the drive may leave data behind.

Some Suggestions

The following is an outline procedure followed by a hardware maintenance provider to minimise such risks.

1. Hard disk drive faults are assigned a unique Customer Reference number (CR) recorded in the Customer Database (CDB). The faulty hard disk drive is securely packaged by the field based engineering personnel and secure courier collection from the practice is arranged for delivery into the goods-in section.

2. All returns are shipped with a fully completed Fault Repair Card, including CDB, CR, Date, Part Serial No., Fault Details, and Engineer's Name.

3. On arrival into the goods-in section, hard disk drives are cross-referenced to their respective CR number and then stored in a locked, secure quarantine area for two weeks.

    The quarantine period allows, for example, data retrieval (or what data can be retrieved) from the replaced hard disk drive should the new disk drive fail prior to a successful full backup.

4. After quarantine hard disk drives undergo low-level format and verification. This procedure is repeated twice.

5. Hard disk drives then undergo full testing by writing then deleting dummy data to each sector on the drive using PC Check Hard Disk Diagnostic software.

    After this process each sector on the hard disk will have been overwritten three times.

6. If the drive fails the test process it is returned to the supplier for a warranty replacement but will have been thoroughly sanitised by this stage.

7. If the drive fails the test process and is out of warranty it is physically dismantled and the data platter destroyed.

Disaster recovery

The Problem

Sometimes an IT system is struck by disaster. The cause may be catastrophic like a flood or fire destroying or severely damaging the IT infrastructure or something more mundane like a prolonged power failure.

Whatever the cause the effect is that the IT systems are either not available or cannot be relied on.

Some Suggestions

Avoiding Disaster

Generally consider the physical issues of the sort we have touched on before. For example, consider detectors and alarms to cover:

- Intruder;
- Water;
- Smoke; or
- Fire.

In addition:

- Check after each installation of equipment that the power supply remains adequate;

- Arrange preventative maintenance for both hardware and software.

Prepare for Disaster

Have a disaster recovery plan – this allows a rapid response to be made after a disaster has struck.

The plan should assist in triage of the IT system after disaster by listing those elements essential to the running of the system and those that can be postponed or even ignored.

Keep a full and up to date inventory of all your IT equipment and software including version numbers where appropriate. It is difficult to recreate a system that is (inevitably) in a state of flux but this becomes virtually impossible when there is no complete record of what that state represents.

The disaster recovery plan should also list vital contacts (including the relevant emergency services) and including:

- equipment and software suppliers;
- telecommunications company;
- insurance company and/or brokers;
- remote back-up site;
- key staff members;
- stand-by site (if any).

Even if you have no formal stand-by site, if there is a true catastrophe you will need alternative premises before any recovery can start.

In addition the plan must give details of access to the back-up store and instructions for recovery of both software and data. Remember it is possible in such circumstances that those who are familiar with the operation of the IT system will not be available to assist in the restoration process. So, any instructions must be complete, detailed and without ambiguity.

Close liaison with your IT supplier before a catastrophe will also be vital. Where this has taken place it is much easier for them to provide replacement equipment. Furthermore, you should consider a legal commitment from the suppliers that they will provide what is required – rather than one based on moral or commercial imperatives or general goodwill.

When drafting your recovery plan also consider:

- Having an off site backup of the disaster recovery plan itself;

- Backup power supply (whether temporary in the form of 'UPS' systems or more permanent in the form of diesel generators) and/or a means of ensuring that protection is available against power peaks and troughs ('power regulators');

- Duplicate or stand by equipment ('redundancy') either on or off-site;

- How (and where) you will be able to retrieve backup media and the equipment to run it on

- Testing the backup media to see: what programs and equipment you need to restore it onto a brand new server/network/client machine from scratch, whether that restore works and the integrity of the restored data. Remember also in this context that there may be licensing implications – the software licence ordinarily may be limited to use on particular machines at particular locations.

Networks

The Problem

The ease with which data may be shared in a networked environment – whether in the same building or in a wider context or even over the Internet – is matched by a danger that the other users of the network may either be unauthorised to see the data or not observe your high standards of data security.

Typical risks range from the 'shared' (and even when applicable usually, not password protected) fax machine, printer, hard drive or directory to the unguarded use of remote access software such as Lap Link or PCAnywhere.

These latter programs, whilst undoubtedly satisfying a need for remote access and containing many security features are often not used carefully and so provide an insecure gateway into what may otherwise be a secure system.

As an example, in March 2002, one of the writers carried out a survey of non-password protected Lap Link or PCAnywhere client machines awaiting connections via the Internet.

At the very first attempt he found a total of 72 such systems. Randomly chosen connections were tested and allowed the writer complete access to the relevant systems as if he were sitting at the relevant machine, logged in and with the password already typed.

Some Suggestions

Network defences include:

- put shared printers (and indeed fax machines) in a secure area so the print outs cannot be intercepted by third parties;

- password protect shared directories (rather than whole drives) and consider hiding them using tools like PGP;

- use a firewall – a combination of hardware and software used to protect the shared data behind the wall;

- use the security facilities in programs like PCAnywhere and Lap Link (password protection, dial back and so on);

- encryption of data on shared drives so unauthorised interlopers will only have access to 'scrambled' data;

- change default system passwords;

- test and try to break your own security or alternatively contract a specialist to do so;

- use secure, for example some NHS related, networks where possible rather than insecure connections over dial up lines.

Passwords

The Problem

Passwords are often one of the weakest links in a security system.

This is because of human frailty and human nature.

Human frailty dictates that it is much easier to remember a date of birth or name of child, spouse or pet than a 12 digit randomly generated alphanumeric code.

Even if 'the management' insists on such a code and bears with fortitude the risk of lock outs and added administration that causes human nature will seek a solution to the memory game – usually in the form of passwords written on yellow sticky labels attached to monitors or on elderly pieces of paper in the top desk drawer on the right.

Some Suggestions

There are a variety of ways in which those seeking to keep data secure can address this problem including:

- education – stressing to the user the crucial value of the password in protecting vital data;

- no multiple use passwords – each person should have their own password and not use a group password;

- access rights – not all users need access to all areas – a decision must be made as to the relevant access level. That decision must be made on the basis of need and not status. The senior partner or consultant does not necessarily 'need' the highest access. The fewer that share it the greater the secret;

- set a minimum length password – say six digits at least – and require this to be changed from time to time (for example monthly – sooner if there is a security breach) and not re-used for a period (for example one year);

- do not allow certain passwords: first names, all numeric, SECRET or PASSWORD;

- where relevant – as in the case of temporary contract workers – issue a time limited password;

- remember that certain software packages – such as Crystal Reports – can bypass application level passwords as well as data level consent settings by directly accessing the database tables. Use of such products must be carefully regulated;

- display a warning screen on the login screen reminding the user of the civil and criminal breaches and the penalties.

Finally, consider the use of biometrics.

For example fingerprint recognition software converts the whorl patterns into an encrypted digital signature that is not only very easy to remember but also extremely secure.

This addresses both issues – human frailty and human nature. After all, very few of us attend work forgetting our right forefinger or allow others to take it in without us.

Security Policy

The Problem

All too often system users either do not appreciate the significance of the data with which they work or their appreciation has been dulled by routine – familiarity breeds contempt.

Some Suggestions

As part of a wider program of security education a security policy may well be critical. BS7799[2] describes a code of practice for information security and proposes that each organisation should have an information policy.

Covered by the policy should be what the BS7799[2] describes as 'ten key controls' namely:

1   Information security policy document
2   Allocation of information security responsibilities
3   Information security education and training
4   Reporting of Security Incidents
5   Virus Controls
6   Business Continuity Planning Process
7   Control of proprietary software copying
8   Safeguarding of organisational records
9   Data Protection
10   ?

For further information and access to an example security policy please refer to *Further Reading*, below.

Screens and Display Boards

The Problem

By their nature and purpose screens are an easy means for the unauthorised to see confidential data.

Some Suggestions

Screens should be placed where they cannot easily be over-looked and users should try to ensure that confidential displays are kept to a minimum.

Relevant steps include:

- not placing screens facing windows, tiled or mirrored surfaces or in the reception area where patients can see them;

---

2.   BS 7799: A Code of Practice for Information Security

- use of overlay screens that restrict the field of view (as well as reducing glare for the user);

- ensure those seeing patients clear the details of the preceding patient from the screen before the next patient enters the room;

- if a patient arrives with others (for example friends or family members) the screen should be shielded from the other people present;

- set a screen saver so the screen will blank when there has been no user action on the keyboard or mouse by the user and only be restored after the user has typed a password.

Similar issues affect waiting area display boards.

Whilst there may be debate as to implied consent of the use of a patient name in such circumstances it may still be safer for express consent to be obtained or for the board to refer to a patient number rather than name especially in the case of famous patients or more than usually confidential reasons for the patient's visit.

Viruses

The Problem

Computer viruses are increasingly common – as at March 2002 at least 60,000 viruses were known to exist either in the wild or in laboratory conditions.

Many of those viruses are intended to cause data corruption or loss and many more do so inadvertently.

Some Suggestions

Whilst the best protection against such viruses is not to 'catch' them (via downloading or otherwise using files from other computers) to enforce such a policy would minimise many of the advantages given by networked computers.

Therefore, a managed risk response to this is as follows:

- ban the running of unauthorised software on the system — in particular games (especially downloaded or from 'cover disks');

- use proprietary virus checking software and keep the data definitions files up to date – preferably weekly but certainly monthly (more often if a particular virus is publicised). This can be set up to run automatically;

- set up a 'sheep dip' – any files that come into the system from elsewhere – whether by download, floppy disk, CD or DVD-Rom or otherwise – should be specifically virus checked. Because these are higher risk files this is better than relying on the less thorough background scanning carried out by most virus software in the hope of balancing security (more through scanning) against convenience (delay whilst scanning takes place);

- for your own reputation's sake, consider a sheep dip for any files you allow to leave your network;

- use a filtering service or product that denies access to potentially dangerous file types such as screen savers that do not have a direct business benefit;

- on discovery or suspicion of a virus: disconnect the infected machine from the network, run a virus detection program on that and other locally networked computers. If a fix (as opposed to deletion) is offered follow the instructions carefully – data is often lost unnecessarily in such circumstances. If in doubt consult your system and/or virus protection supplier before taking drastic steps.

Caldicott recommendations

The Caldicott Committee Report[3] on the review of patient-identifiable information made a number of recommendations that are of interest here. We do not apologise that these emphasise by repetition some of the points we have already made.

---

3.   Caldicott Report (The Caldicott Committee Report on the Review of Patient – Identifiable Information, December 1997, NHS Executive, London. See Appendix 3.

Basic Server security

Users should be made aware that sharing of passwords or network user identities is the easiest method of gaining access to information to which one is not authorised to access.

So, users should be advised:

- To keep all passwords in a safe place
- To keep the server "locked" at all times.

Patient Consent

The system must show comprehensively:

- which parts of their data the patient has given permission to be viewed,

- by whom, and

- for what reasons.

This must be capable of being modified – if a patient changes their mind this date will be essential in auditing what was available for viewing at what date (pre- and post-consent).

The audit must show who registered this change in permission.

The existence of suppressed data should be flagged – it might be pertinent to future diagnosis and this should also be indicated if likely to be the case.

Reasons for accessing a record include:

- Access to parts of the records created by the person seeking access,
- With implied patient consent,
- With express patient consent,
- In the patient's best interest,
- In the public interest,
- Required by law, or
- In response to a patient's access request.

Patients may have direct access to various parts of their records.

Supplier Services – Support and Training

The supplier must demonstrate that further documentation exists to support a confidentiality clause in the contract with the practice, and that this is made available to all staff.

This must include:

- An employment contract for all new staff and, where possible, for all existing staff, which underlines the importance of respecting the confidentiality of patient data and states that any breach of confidentiality is likely to lead to summary dismissal. If it is not possible to change the contracts of existing staff to include such a clause, the documentation must include an agreement which they are required to sign, covering the same information.

- Similar agreements must also be available for all subcontractors and agents who may come into contact with any sensitive data.

Internal procedures must be in place for dealing with access to all data relating to patients and to the business of the practice, which cover:

- Code of conduct for visiting practices.
- Procedures for handling confidential data in paper reports.
- Procedures for handling tapes and disks.
- Procedures for remote support.

Documentation

The system documentation must specify the security measures of the system.

The following items must be drawn to the attention of the user, as good practice, in training or other documentation:

- Passwords should contain at least one non-alphabetic character;

- Passwords should not be embedded in function keys and macros;

- Instructions should be included on what to do, and who to consult, on failed login.

The system documentation must refer to other relevant publications which detail additional security management requirements on staff.

The system documentation must remind the practice of the importance of complying with the Data Protection Act 1998 requirement to include information about security standards in their Data Protection registration.

The system documentation must remind users of the importance of complying with the recommendations in the Caldicott Report and should advise practices to seek the advice of their local Caldicott Guardian on any matter relating to the confidentiality of patient identifiable data.

The system documentation must remind users of the importance of complying with other relevant legislation, notably the Regulation of Investigatory Powers Act 2000 and the Electronic Communications Act 2000.

The system documentation must remind users of the importance of seeking the appropriate level of informed consent of the patient before making any data available to a third party.

Example Confidentiality Clause

The following is an example of a clause on confidentiality for inclusion in a system supplier support contract:

We (the supplier) acknowledge that when providing support services we may have access to confidential data in relation to your practice and patients.

We agree to keep access to such information limited to that strictly necessary to provide our support services and to keep any such information confidential.

When we take copies of data for support purposes we will only do so with your consent, keeping such data secure and returning or destroying it as soon as possible. We will destructively erase any data held on any media removed from your system in the course of maintenance as soon as practicable. Our staff have been made aware of the importance of respecting the confidentiality of your data and that summary dismissal is the likely consequence of failing to do so.

Email/Internet Policy

As a consequence of the Regulation of Investigatory Powers Act 2000 (and the regulations made under it), the Data Protection Act 1998 and the Human Rights Act 1998 it is now more important than ever for every organisation to have an Email/Internet policy.

Not only that but the policy must be publicised, explained and enforced.

The following is adapted, as an example, for use by a general medical practice:

E-Mail Policy

The Practice has an e-mail system which is intended to promote the Practice's activities by making communication more effective. The Practice may be liable if the system is misused by, for example, defamatory messages being sent to third parties through the e-mail system. The e-mail system is not meant for personal messages and they should be avoided so far as is possible. The following rules are applicable:

1. The language and content of any messages must be of an appropriate standard and should be succinct and to the point.

2. Inappropriate language which may include malicious gossip or messages that may amount to a breach of the Practice's equal opportunity policies or be otherwise inappropriate will be treated as a disciplinary offence.

3. Confidential information must not be sent by e-mail.

4. E-mail sent through the Practice system shall be, become and remain the property of the Practice and the Practice shall have the right to retrieve all e-mails for such reasons as it considers appropriate.

5. If you receive an e-mail for which you were not the intended recipient you should immediately notify the sender. If you, yourself, receive an e-mail that is not considered to contain appropriate matter you should notify your Manager.

6. Deliberate or knowing misuse of the e-mail system may constitute gross misconduct and the Practice will not tolerate the sending of e-mails that are malicious, untrue, obscene or defamatory. The Practice will operate its disciplinary procedures in respect of any such misuse.

7. You should not open unsolicited e-mail if you do not know its source because it may contain a virus. You must immediately report receipt of such e-mail to [........].

Adapted from *Contracts of Employment*,
M. Duggan, EMIS Professional Publishing 2001

Turning to the Internet itself the following comes from EMIS Legal's Law for Doctors electronic book on Employment Law: Seneca EP, *Law for Doctors*, 2002, EMIS Professional Publishing.

The Internet

We know that a large volume of pornographic and unsuitable material appears on the web. It can be accessed quite innocently in some cases by accessing search engines with quite innocent word searches.

However it has been clear in the past that employees have deliberately accessed pornographic and/or unsuitable sites.

Anyone found accessing, downloading, distributing, reading or otherwise any such sites will be subject to the disciplinary procedure – such conduct being regarded as gross misconduct for which summary dismissal is one possible outcome.

Anyone who innocently accesses an unsuitable site should report this immediately to his/her line manager.

The Practice has introduced software that has the capacity for detecting unsuitable and pornographic material. It prevents any such access and identifies the person seeking access. Strict disciplinary measures will be taken against anyone found to have attempted to accessed such sites/materials.

As you would expect, anyone caught attempting to or accessing paedophilic material on the web will be subject to summary dismissal (following a disciplinary hearing) and the police will be called on every occasion.

I hope that you all will behave responsibly with our email and Internet facilities.

These rules will apply whether you are accessing the web during your lunch hour or other meal breaks paid or unpaid or outside normal working hours.

Conclusion

We leave you with a final section by way of further reference and remind you of these words:

'What can't be avoided must be endured'

We hope that these, necessarily brief, suggestions are of assistance in both avoiding and enduring data loss.

Further reference

- The Handbook of Information Security, NHS Executive's Information Management Group, E5209 May 1995.

- Ensuring Security and Confidentiality in NHS Organisations, a Resource Pack, NHS Executive's Security and Data Protection Programme, E5501 January 1999.

- *Email, the Internet and the Law* Kevan & McGrath, EMIS Professional Publishing 2001

- *Data Protection Law* David Bainbridge, EMIS Professional Publishing 2000

- *Contracts of Employment* Michael Duggan, EMIS Professional Publishing 2001

- The EMIS Legal, *Law for Doctors*, Employment Law E-book, EMIS Professional Publishing 2002

CHAPTER 6
PATIENT CONFIDENTIALITY:
THE TRUST PERSPECTIVE

Robert McSherry, Principal Lecturer, Teeside University,
Paddy Pearce, Clinical Governance Manager, Friarage Hospital, Northallerton and
Dr Richard Griffin, MREP, Consultant Physician, Chichester

Introduction

When patients attend their local hospital trust they expect to be treated with privacy, respect and dignity and that any information disclosed during consultation with any health and social care personnel will be treated in the strictest of confidence. "Everyone working for the NHS has a legal duty to keep information about you confidential".[1] The chapter outlines why confidentiality is important to NHS organisations and individual healthcare personnel by providing a practical framework for raising awareness of the issues associated with confidentiality and record keeping. Confidentiality is defined and related to the latest policy documents and guidance issued by the Department of Health (DoH) and professional bodies. The importance of confidentiality within the clinical governance framework is explored and its relevance to maintaining high standards of record and record keeping. The significance of patient data/information and how it is aggregated into healthcare information in influencing policy changes is explored.

---

1. Department of Health (1999) *The Protection and Use of Patient Information: Guidance from the Department of Health* DOH, London. *http://www.doh.gov.uk/confiden/pguide6.htm*

Why confidentiality is important to an NHS Trust

Over the past decade since the publications of the Patients Charter[2] and the Code of Openness of the NHS[3] there has been an increased awareness of patient's rights to health and social care. The publication of the Access to Medical Reports Act[4] and Access to Health Records Act[5] has further reinforced patient's rights to information held about them in health and social care records. "Records" in this instance refer to any form of information with the patient's identity held on it such as computer data basis, patient administration systems and written health and social care notes. Easier access to information via the Internet and media coverage of health and social care issues reinforces the need to protect disclosures of information about patients and staff. All information should be viewed and treated with the strictest of confidence and sensitivity. Disclosure of information should only be made with the permission and consent of the individual concerned. Where confidentiality has been breached patients are more likely to seek redress through the courts.[6] Confidentiality is an integral part of the professional's unique relationship with the patient. Fear of disclosure of private and sensitive information could result in a professional/patient relationship that may affect the patient's treatment. If the patient's trust of the professional is impinged due to a lack or breach of confidence in the way information was obtained, stored or subsequently used, actions may be taken by the relevant professional bodies.[7]

The professional bodies such as the General Medical Council (GMC)[8] and the United Kingdom Central Council for Nursing, Midwifery and Health Visiting (UKCC)[9] known toady as the new Nursing Midwifery Council (NMC) have incorporated confidential within their codes of conduct and as such deem breaches of confidential as a breach of the professional code. The difficulty for some health and social care professionals and supporting staff is in defining and applying the principles of confidentiality into their daily practice.

2.   Department of Health (1992) *Patients Charter: Raising the Standard* HMSO, London.
3.   Department of Health (1997) *Code of Openness in the NHS* HMSO, London.
4.   Access to Medical Reports Act 1998 London, HMSO
5.   Access to Health Records Act 1990 London, HMSO
6.   McSherry R, Pearce P (2002) *Clinical Governance A Guide To Implementation For HealthCare Professionals* Blackwell Science Publishers, Oxford.
7.   Blanchard H (1999) Duty of Confidence? *Health Care Risk Report* 5, 9, 12–13
8.   General Medical Council (2000) *Confidentiality: Protecting and Providing Information* GMC, London.
9.   United Kingdom Council for Nursing, Midwifery and Health Visiting (1996) Guidelines for Professional Practice. UKCC, London.

Defining what we mean by confidentiality

Confidentially is defined as "Secret; private; in confidence. Entrusted with private matters".[10] A definition, which at face value, seems to be concerned with personal interactions and not the recording of such events or consultations. Confidentiality within health and social care goes beyond the interactions between patients and staff in maintaining privacy and dignity but demands that records are kept of all such events in the strictest of confidence. Information or data recorded as part of the patient's health or social care experience(s) should only be used for the purposes of providing proper care, treatment and follow ups. Information may be disclosed where the public are at risk of infectious or communicable diseases, to support research and the education of staff that may benefit the public. The law and professional bodies may request information pertinent to a legal or professional case.[11] To ensure that confidentiality is maintained it is essential that health and social care staff working for a trust or social care organisation are informed of the importance of confidentiality. Similarly patients too should be informed of their rights of confidentiality. The education and training of issues akin to confidentiality should be an integral part of all induction programmes and be based upon current guidelines issues from the government, professional or voluntary organisations.

New Policy Documents and their Relevance

For more information, see Chapter 4.

The significant guidance and policy documents for NHS staff to be aware of on the use of confidential information can be classified into three main areas: government policy, professional standards and user involvement. The government's strategy for improving confidentiality within health and social care is highlighted through the publication of the Health Service Guidance (HSG) 1996/18 *The Protection and Use of Patient Information*[12] and the Caldicott Report.[13] The HSG 1996/18 informed the development of the Caldicott Committee with the aim of reviewing "all patient identifiable information that passes between NHS organisations and other non NHS bodies for purposes other than direct care, medical research or where there is statutory requirement for

---

10. Collins W (1987) *Collins Universal English Dictionary* Readers Union Ltd. Glasgow.

11. National Health Services Executive (1999) *The Protection And Use of Patient Information: Guidance from the Department of Health – Annex A.* DoH, London.

12. National Health Service Executive (1996) *Health Service Guidance 1996/18 'The Protection and Use of Patient Information'* DoH, London.

13. Department of Health (1999) *The Caldicott Report* DoH, London. *See Appendix 2.*

such data".[14] These documents provide clear information and guidance on how confidential information should be used within and external to the NHS through the adoption of six good practice principles.

Practice principles which states that patient identifiable information should be justified and only used when it is absolutely necessary where the information is kept to a minimum. Access to such information should be on a strict need to know basis where staff take full responsibility in understanding their actions when disclosing information and in complying with the law. For example, are staff aware of the Data Protection Act[15] and that patients have a right to review their personnel healthcare records? Disclosures of information without permission and the patient discovering could lead to legal action.

The Caldicott Report provides sixteen recommendations surrounding the use of patient identifiable information (see Appendix 2). The key points for trusts and healthcare employees to be aware off is that a senior person, preferably a healthcare professional, should be made responsible for safeguarding patient information. This post is currently referred to as the Caldicott Guardian. A strategy for reinforcing confidentiality and information security through ongoing education and training of staff should be introduced along with clear policies and guidelines for staff to access and follow for the release of information within and external to the organisation. Similarly a strategy for informing users of health and social care of their rights and responsibilities surrounding confidentiality should be undertaken. Likewise, staff should be informed of the role of the Patient Information Advisory Group in safeguarding patients. The PSAG is outlined in detail later in the section at page 119.

The professional bodies, the GMC and the NMC, provide explicit guidance for the protection and disclosure of patient information outlining the responsibilities of healthcare professionals. It is imperative that all healthcare professionals avail themselves of the guidance issued by their own specific professional bodies and that this is reflected in the trust local policies or guidance on confidentiality and contracts of employment. As a matter of good practice we would suggest that all health and social care organisations include a confidentiality clause within contracts of employment and in any policy standards for record and record keeping.

As part of the NHS modernisation agenda we have witnessed a unique approach to ensuring patient consultation and involvement in policy

14. National Health Service Executive (1999) *Draft Consultation Paper – Caldicott Guardians* DoH, London.

15. UK Parliament (1998) Data Protection Act HMSO, London.

developments of the NHS. In keeping with the philosophy of user involvement as outlined in the National Plan[16] several initiatives have been pursued in order to involve users of NHS services. The National Confidential and Security Advisory Body (NCSAB)[17] was formed in March 2000 with the remit of:

- Setting national standards to govern the confidentiality and security of patient information;

- Promote awareness of issue surrounding patients records, including access and security;

- Feed guidance to, and provide support for, the 'Caldicott Guardians';

- Advise ministers, the DoH and the NHS Information Authority on a wide range of confidentiality and security issues.

However, the NCSAB was never formally launched within the NHS. What has emerged is the Patient Information Advisory Group (PIAG) with a remit of *"representing patient groups, healthcare professionals and regulatory bodies, will make sure patients rights are maintained when the NHS and other health related organisations use medical information about patients"*.[18] By extension we would argue that the PIAG covers all health and social care information if it is to successfully operate in balancing section 60 of the Health and Social Care Act. Section 60

> "provides a power to ensure that patient identifiable information needed to support essential NHS activity can be used without the consent of patients. The power can only be used to support medical purposes that are in the interests of patients or the wider public, where consent is not a practicable alternative and where anonymised information will not suffice. It is intended largely as a transitional measure whilst consent or anonymisation procedures are developed, and this is reinforced by the need to review each of its powers annually".[19]

16.   Department of Health (2000) *The National Plan A Plan for Reform A Plan for Investment* HMSO, London.

17.   Department of Health (2000) *New body to advise on patient confidentiality* DoH, London.

18.   Department of Health (2001) *Health Minister announces group to advise on use of patient information*. DoH London.

19.   Department of Health (2001) The Health and Social Care Act 2001: Section 60 and 61 Background Information.

Essentially section 60 endorses the principles of the Caldicott Report. To ensure that patient identifiable information is appropriately used the PIAG has been established as part of Section 60 and could also be seen as a guardian for ensuring the use of patient information. NHS Trust should familiarise themselves with the role of PIAG and how to access its services in the use of patient information to support service developments. PIAG information can be found on the following Web Sites:

Department of Health (2001) *Health Minister announces group to advise on use of patient information.* DoH London
www.doh.gov.uk/ipu/confiden/act/piagannounce/htm

Department of Health (2001) The Health and Social Care Act 2001: Section 60 and 61 Background Information.
www.doh.gov.uk/ipu/confiden/act/s60bg.htm

Department of Health (2001) PIAG Terms of Reference DoH, London
www.doh.gov.uk/ipu/confiden/act/tor.htm

National Health Service England and Wales (2001) Statutory Instruments No 2836 Patient Information Advisory Group (Establishment) Regulations DoH, HMSO.
www.hmso.gov.uk/si/si2001/20012836.htm

The introduction of the PIAG could be attributed to awareness in the NHS of a growing lack of public confidence in the safeguarding of patient information. Advances in healthcare informatics and technology is making information easier to record, store and access in a variety of formats such as Electronic Patient Held Records, Pathways of Care and Clinical Information Systems.

There is a growing interest in patient information held by NHS trusts from external organisations such as the Public Health Laboratory Services (an organisation responsible for collating health and social care data notably around communicable and infectious diseases) and by the patients themselves. The Patient Information Advisory Group is needed to provide advice and guidance to Ministers on how the request for confidential information should be considered in the future.

Confidential and security of information is everyone's business and as such patients should have their say. The recording of health and social care information is the responsibility of all employees from the Chief Executive to the Domestic; a point echoed by Gisela Stuart, Minister for Health "safeguarding confidential patient information is the responsibility of everybody who works in the NHS".[20] Patients have a right to expect the highest of standards from clinical and non-clinical staff regarding the confidentiality of their records and record keeping in demonstrating that they have received quality care. Maintaining high standards of record and record keeping is essential and the only way to demonstrate the quality of care provided at an individual, team and organisational level. Confidentiality associated with records and record keeping should be intergraded within the clinical governance frameworks.

Examining confidentiality within the clinical governance framework

Clinical governance defined as 'a protective mechanism for the public and healthcare professionals, ensuring that their local hospitals and community trusts are actively developing structures to improve the quality of care".[21] Clinical governance is an umbrella term for all the issues and concepts that clinicians know and foster, including standard setting, risk management, continuous quality improvement, continuing professional development, evidence based practice and communication and information.[22] Clinical governance can be conceptualised into five key components:

- quality improvement and maintenance;
- professional and organisational accountability;
- culture;
- safety; and
- information.

These components in turn could be considered as the building blocks for its success for an individual, team or organisation. For clinical governance to operate effectively these components need to be evident and operational. Confidentiality is an integral part of clinical governance because the systems and processes are founded upon the principals of effective communication and the way information is

20. Department of Health (2000) *New body to advise on patient confidentiality* DoH, London.
21. Smith R (1998) All changed, changed utterly: British Medicine will be transformed by the Bristol Case *BMJ* 316, 1917–18.
22. McSherry R, & Haddock J (1999) Evidence based health care: its place within clinical governance *British Journal of Nursing* 8 (2) 113–117.

collected, monitored, stored and audited. Information storage and retrieval are imperative in demonstrating the efficiency and effectiveness of the key components of clinical governance, which are also governed by the same policies and laws associated with safeguarding patient information and records. The difficulty health and social organisations are having is in linking confidentiality to the systems and processes required to demonstrate effective governance. Effective governance at an organisational level can only be demonstrated by the collection and aggregation of patient held information examples being mortality rates, infectious diseases, readmission rates, length of bed occupancy, staff sickness and absence rate etc... Information disclosed related to these matters must not be patient or staff specific, thus leading to a breach of confidentiality. To avoid breaching confidentiality of patient information health and social care organisations – under the umbrella of clinical governance – need to establish efficient and effective processes for monitoring and auditing standards of records and record keeping.

There are several practical approaches available to auditing the standards of records and record keeping in ensuring the confidentiality of patient information within health and social care records such as those provided by the Clinical Negligence Scheme for Trusts (CNST)[23] and the Medical Defence Union (MDU).[24] The CNST standards associated with records and keeping provide in-depth practical guidance relating to the achievement of predetermined standards. The standards provided are universal, generic, adaptable and objective in demonstrating the effectiveness of written records for the multidisciplinary team within health and social care. The standards focus on issues such as: access and security to records, accuracy of the recorded entries of patient information and a means for auditing the effectiveness of the written records. The MDU's legal advisor Dr. Nicolas Norwell provides a informed approach in an article entitled 'Thou shalt tell the truth' highlighting the principals of good practice for the standards of recording, storing and disclosing patient information based around the ten commandments. Dr. Norwell article provides valuable information relating to confidentiality and records.

Based upon the works of the CNST and MDU it is imperative that health and social care organisations design a strategic and structured approach to maintaining and improving patient confidentiality and the way information is documented through the standards of record and record keeping. Clinical governance, can be seen to already

23.   National Health Service Litigation Authority (2001) Clinical Negligence Scheme for Trusts Manual of Standards. NHSLA, Bristol.

24.   Norwell N (1996) *Thou shalt tell the truth, says the MDU*, Medical Defence Union, 1997 vol. 13 no. 1, London.

support the strategic development of ensuring confidentiality and quality records and record keeping because the systems and processes required to design, monitor and evaluate the standards of record and record keeping are already available. To be achieving clinical governance you must by definition, already have a good communications system. If there is a suspected breach of patient confidentiality or identified poor standards of record keeping the incident or complaint should be reviewed by the application of the established clinical governance framework. The framework should be applied to establish the facts surrounding the whole incident/complaint. The quality improvement agenda incorporating risk management should critically review the untoward clinical incident or complaint, focusing on whether confidentiality has been breached. It must also review the standard of record keeping in light of the standards previously set for documenting information. The critical review may highlight poor practices at an individual, team or organisational level in the way patient information is stored and disclosed. The potential outcome of such an incident is that an organisational approach to sustaining confidentiality of patient information is required along with the establishment of a written policy and standards for auditing of confidentiality and records and record keeping along with the education and training of personnel.

The Audit Commission Report *Data Remember*[25] stresses the importance of improving the quality of patient-based information in the NHS and how it relates to the planning, provision and highlighting performance of the services. The Audit Commission Report provides practical advice and guidance on how the quality of patient information is the bedrock to demonstrating successful patient outcomes. To assure patient confidentiality and a high standard of record keeping within the clinical governance framework it is essential that health and social care trusts familiarise themselves with this document.

Conclusion

Confidentiality can no longer be viewed in isolation but should be seen as an integral part of maintaining and improving the quality of health and social care. Within clinical governance confidentiality should be embedded within the key components so that any patient information acquired as a result of interactions with health or social care is valued and treated with sensitivity and the strictest of confidence. Disclosure

---

25.   The Audit Commission (2002) *Data Remember* Audit Commission, London.

of patient identifiable information should only occur where the patients give their informed consent or when the professional body or law requires. Health and social care trusts should endeavour to assist the Caldicott Guardians in the execution of their role and responsibilities in safeguarding patient information by adhering to the principals of high standards of record and record keeping. To accommodate the challenges of a 21st century society within a modernising NHS, health and social care trusts need to ensure that personnel are informed of the relevant information about confidentiality and records and record keeping. Essential to this process is raising awareness through formal education and training programmes explicit in informing staff of:

- why confidentiality is important,

- what confidentiality means,

- highlighting important policies and documents and

- how confidentiality relates to clinical governance.

CHAPTER 7
AN INDIVIDUAL GP'S CONCERNS
ABOUT PATIENT CONFIDENTIALITY

Mary Hawking, Senior Partner, Kingsbury Court Surgery

Introduction

This chapter provides a GP's perspective on the confidentiality issues facing practices. Key questions are raised – not all of which can be answered yet from the legal or governance materials published so far.

The Good (or Bad) Old Days

My practice became computerised in 1992, and at that time life seemed fairly simple – at anyrate, as far as holding electronic records was concerned.

There appeared to be two pieces of legislation which were relevant – the Data Protection Act 1984 and possibly the Computer Misuse Act 1990.

Everything else regarding Confidentiality was governed by a combination of common law duty and guidance from the GMC – and I suspect most doctors didn't have much difficulty with this approach.

Of course, theoretically, holding *anything* only on the computer was technically a breach of Terms of Service (TOS). TOS stated that GP medical records must be held on " stationary supplied by the Secretary of State for Health". *Did* this include the right hand side of computer generated prescriptions? I don't know.. and I never heard of anyone being disciplined for breaching this rule...

However, things change – and not only in the NHS. Who could have predicted not only the technical development of IT since 1990, making routine analysis and widespread distribution of large amounts of data possible, but also the fall in cost of the technology, making it feasible in the NHS?

The development of the technology allowed the development of plans that depended crucially on the application of that technology and wide-spread sharing of patient information – both individually identifiable and pseudo or totally anonymised – for direct patient care and for management and research purposes.

Identifiable patient information has always been shared to some extent: without some degree of sharing, it wouldn't be possible to care for patients or run the business of the NHS. Even before the Internal Market (1990 – 1998) it was necessary to know not only how many hernia operations had been performed, but also on whom the procedures had been done. The difference now appears to be the range of people and organisations expecting to share my patients' medical records, and the extent of the information expected. My patient might not be concerned about everyone in the NHS knowing he had a hernia operation – but this does not mean that he is equally unconcerned about revealing the rest of his not necessarily sordid history. Having no problems with sharing information with other doctors and clinicians within the NHS does not necessarily mean that he is happy to have it shared with other organisations, when he has not been consulted either about sharing his information or the purposes for which it might be used.

Developments since 1992

The original IMG[1] Strategy was published in 1992 – and was broadly welcomed at the time: this dealt mainly with infrastructure – NHS Number, NHSNet, the NHS Tracing System, Coding – both Read Code and ICD (International Classification of Disease) – and use of EDIFACT for Pathology messaging.

Confidentiality issues *were* mentioned – but, at that time, the means of breaching confidentiality and the ever-increasing demands for patient identifiable information for purposes such as NHS management, research and "joined up care" (which implies that

---

1.   Information Management Group – replaced by the NHS Information Authority (NHSIA).

information will be shared with other partner organisations) were not as important as the infrastructure.

Since then, things have changed. The technology has developed, so that sharing information is possible – and, in many settings, routine. Both within the NHS and in other organisations, the general climate regarding confidentiality and the uses to which information, given for one purpose, may legitimately be used for other purposes has changed. In medical circles, there has been sometimes heated debate about the need for explicit or implied consent for such use, and there are also differences of opinion about what constitutes express and implied consent, and what amount of information is covered by either.

Since 1997, the pace of change has increased and problems still remain. The main issues relate to consent and confidentiality.[2]

Consent – what is it?

Guidance has been issued on obtaining fully informed consent – but this seems to relate to procedures and treatment – not to consent for release of information.

Even when a patient agrees to release of information, is the consent fully informed if they are not aware of the further uses to which information may be put, or the amount of information they have agreed to release?

For instance, patients may be aware that they have given consent for release of the whole medical record for a Life Insurance application, but not be aware that the same amount of information has been requested by a solicitor for a claim or case involving a minor accident.

What is Implied Consent – and how far does this extend?

If the NHS decides that, in the interests of running the NHS, patients giving any information to a clinician should expect that this information may be used for administration and epidemiology, and, after public consultation – due, I understand, in the summer of 2002, – should the public expect this to include use for commercially sponsored clinical trials, and sharing with all the government departments mentioned in the Information Policy Unit (IPU)

---

2. For more on the statutory and legal background, see Part I above. For more on the clinical governance background, see Part II above. For background, history and further reading, see Further Reading at page 138.

discussion[3] document launched in April 2002? What happens if an individual wants to opt out?

Information involving more than one person

The classic example of this is the "Child at Risk" case report.

This arrives on my desk with a solomn warning that the contents are confidential and must not be shared without the consent of the issuing body. I agree with that – these case reports involve a number of individuals – the original case, siblings (and, very often, half and step siblings sometimes in several households) and a variety of adults with responsibility or contact with the index child.

My problem is *what do I do with the report?* Particularly if the other individuals are not patients in the practice, and when the child leaves the practice.

Do I mark the child's – and any other vulnerable individual's – EPR with something like "see report in shoe box"? And whose record should it go into? What would be the effect if – in a cradle-to-grave record – the middle-aged patient finds the records of a childhood child at risk conference – by now in a totally different social context? And yet, if the warning does *not* go with the EPR, there would be no indication that the child had ever been considered to be at risk – or that the adults involved might bear watching.

I don't know how to manage this with a paper based record – it isn't just a problem with the EPR. Where do I stand, and what should I do?

The other classic case is family history and now genetic information.

If a patient reports that a relative has some inherited disorder with possible financial consequences – say Huntingdon's Chorea (unlikely to be offered life insurance without a negative genetic test) – should other relatives be accorded the same family history?

It is possible that the original informant was wrong... but even if they were correct, relationships may not be what they appear on paper (there is adoption – and the milkman!)

---

3.   *url for IPU discussion on Information Sharing between Government Departments.*

Genetic information may, in a few cases, identify carriers of genes known to be associated with specific diseases: many of these will be a predisposition rather than a certainty: does this information – often gathered as part of a research or even police enquiry – constitute part of the EPR,[4] and if so, should it be treated in the same way as other information in the EPR? If not, how, in the days of universally available and transferable EPRs could it be protected, legally, ethically and technically?

Technical, Organisational and Legal Developments

There have been a lot of technical as well as organisational and legal developments since the disagreements between the BMA and Department of Health in the early 1990s. I am not sure whether these affect my professional and ethical position – they certainly have a potential effect on my ability to preserve total confidentiality for my patients.

Even in the era of the all encompassing, comprehensive, instantly available EPR envisioned in Information for Health, it seems likely that this will be co-ordinated and maintained largely in or through General Practice – where 90% of patient encounters with Health Care are stated to occur. So the GP will remain responsible, legally and ethically, for preserving – or breaching – the patient's confidentiality.

GPs are not only doctors – they are partners, managing directors, Caldicott Guardians and Security managers within their practices. Doctors in other branches of medicine work in organisations, and responsibility for breaches are likely to lie with the organisation rather than the individual. In general practice, as currently organised (2002), the two are the same.

Technical aspects

Taking a GP point of view, it used to be said that Patient Confidentiality was guaranteed by the Lloyd George envelope and doctor's handwriting – and there was a great deal of truth in that concept.

Since the early 1980s, general practice has become increasingly computerised, and with the introduction of the "new contract" in 1990, and the NHS Plan and Information for Health practices are under a great deal of pressure to hold increasing amounts of patient

---

4.   Electronic Patient Record.

information on computer. This is partly for mundane financial reasons such as claiming for services performed and for clinical and organisational management issues such as audit, and direct patient care – in fact, many of the demands placed on general practice would be difficult if not impossible to fulfil *without* a computerised patient record. Computerised patient records can improve patient care and even doctors' job satisfaction (just think of pre-computer repeat prescribing routines). They also increase the ease of access to patient information – and the risks of accidental or systematic breaches of confidentiality.

I am an enthusiastic supporter of computerised medical records and am in a paperless practice – but there are consequences and potential risks to patient confidentiality that need to be addressed.

Outside access

The sophisticated systems used to maintain modern GP EPRs require maintenance and support – and this means that there has either to be a means of remote access (as in EMIS) or an acceptance that if a fault occurs, it will be necessary for someone to visit the site to effect repair – with potential loss of time and inability to access information which may be vital for patient care. In either case, inevitably, non-clinical individuals have access to the patient database.

A relationship of trust is necessary between any organisation and the supplier where IT is concerned – but the mere existence of authorised remote access means that there is a potential for unauthorised remote access:

- Could a supplier be forced to extract data from a GP system with or without the agreement of the practice concerned? For example, will any regulations under section 60 of the Health and Social Care Act 2001 allow or even mandate this?

- Would a Strategic Health Authority, PCO (Primary Care Organisation), Regional Health Authority – or security service – be able to access my system and extract information?

- And then there's hacking! I may have been reading too much about the skills of hackers – but it is a topic which concerns many GPs!

NHSNet connections

Most GP practices have been connected to the NHSNet and via this to the Internet but how good is the security? And does NHSNet have the same commitment as GPs to preserving confidentiality – or, indeed, do all users agree as to what is meant by "confidentiality"? Very few GPs (or patients) subscribe to the DoH view that the NHS is one big, happy family, and by implication, consent has been given to sharing information given in confidence to the GP with the rest of the NHS. Cain and Abel were brothers, after all!

There has been a good deal of concern about the configuration of the firewalls – or even whether any firewalls were installed in some areas – giving rise to fears that the patient database might be totally exposed.

Central Servers

There is an ongoing debate about whether in the near or distant future GP records, currently held in individual surgeries, will be held on or copied to central servers. What are the implications for control of and access to the data so held – especially if one of the reasons for this configuration was to enable wide access to the individual patient record? Ross Anderson[5] pointed out that large databases are more risky than multiple distributed ones.

Structures to support enforcement of confidentiality

Many of the issues involved are to do with organisation rather than technology. From a GP point of view, there appears to be a lack of appreciation of the fact that releasing information into an environment where I have little confidence in the will, let alone the ability, to maintain patient confidentiality as I understand it, is likely to prevent me maintaining a full medical record – or encourage me to return to the Lloyd George envelope!

After reading this, I am beginning to wonder whether the Lloyd George envelope wasn't PET (privacy enhancing technology) before its time!

---

5.   EPR – Electronic Patient Record was originally used for the GP computer record used to manage the individual patient and potentially replace the paper record completely: *Information for Health* uses EPR as the Acute Trust partial record, EHR – Electronic Health Record – as the total record, including (I think) the social services experiences of the patient.. and I'm not sure where that leaves the good, old-fashioned GP EPR! I'm using EPR here to mean the GP EPR.

Disease Registers, Decision Support, Clinical Governance, PRIMIS and PROFESS

There are a number of other areas where there is a potential for data to be extracted from the practice database in a systematic manner, to assist in audits, improvement of data quality, establishment of PCO[6] wide audits and other such probably worthy causes.

MIQUEST[7] – which was a requirement for RFA accreditation – was designed to allow data to be extracted from different GP systems as truly anonymised data – removing all identifiers – and was used like this in the CHDGP (Collection of Health Data from General Practice) pilot, which was succeeded by PRIMIS[8], with an even greater emphasis on encouraging training in the improvement of data quality.

I find no problem with this, provided the data extracted is truly anonymised, and the practice has the ability and willingness to check each query before it is implemented.

There is, however, a potential for abuse.

Recently a PCO asked nurses helping practices with CHD (Coronary Heart Disease) to extract information about patients with mental health problems, to provide data for a mental health framework action plan without the knowledge or consent of the participating practices. This would seem to suggest a difference in understanding of the legal and ethical aspects of patient confidentiality between the PCO and the practice involved. How widespread is this?

Disease Registers

These are centrally held Registers of patients with a particular condition such as Cancer and Diabetes. They are used for epidemiological research (in the case of Cancer) and additionally for patient management (in the case of Diabetes Mellitus).

There is a very strong feeling among some epidemiologists that only identifiable patient data is valid, and that the value of their work would be impaired if patients were allowed to simply opt out of the Register.

---

6.   PCO – Primary Care Organisation – includes PCTs (Primary Care Trusts) and PCGs (Primary Care Groups); in future will include Care Trusts – PCTs combined with Social Care.
7.   MIQUEST – software language to generate health care queries. For more, see *www.clinical-info.co.uk/miquest.htm.*
8.   PRIMIS – Primary Care Information System.

All the data from the Cancer Register is passed to the National Office of Statistics (NOS), without any anonymisation. I do not know the procedures for protecting confidentiality at the NOS!

Are Disease Registers A Good Thing? I'll pass on that – although it is hard to see how patients with Diabetes, for instance, can be offered the full range of services available if there is not some form of local or central Disease Register – but, if there is a Disease Register, how much information should it contain?

Should patients be asked for consent for their names to be included? Legally, they probably should. Whether they would be willing to be on such a Register probably depends on the perceived advantages – or disadvantages – to the individual patient – and the lack of highly publicised breaches of confidence.

If patients refused to be included, the Registers would not be all inclusive, and therefore less valuable for research and epidemiological purposes.

There is a practical advantage to Diabetic patients in being on a register: there is an ethical advantage to patients with cancer. I am not convinced that the patients with serious mental health problems, the elderly and patients with CHD would necessarily feel the same...

Could I, as a GP, be forced to submit a patient's name for inclusion in a Disease Register, with or without consent? Possibly, under Section 60 of the Health and Social Care Act 2001 – and where does *that* leave my professional obligations?

Decision Support, Clinical Governance, PRIMIS and PROFESS

I'm going to group all of these together: the concern here is that programs and technologies, designed for other purposes, could be used in a manner that breaches individual patient confidentiality.

As always, there is a value judgement here: is the benefit for the individual GP – and his/her patients – of improving patient care (and doctor competence!) by using decision support systems (by this I mean systems integrated with the patient record – such as Prodigy – rather than, as it were, look up facilities like the electronic BNF (British National Formulary), Mentor and Dermis) outweighed by the fact that the use of these systems could – possibly – be used to extract patient data without the knowledge or consent of the practice? Schemes such as PRIMIS and PROFESS explicitly extract patient data – in the case of PRIMIS in a truly anonymised form.

PRIMIS[9] extracts data to provide feed-back to the individual practice and improve the quality of the GP record. This is very valuable – I have strong doubts about the quality of information in many records, both electronic and paper – but this information could be used for other purposes. Provided it remains anonymised, individual patient confidentiality should not be breached.

PROFESS is a research project designed to extract records of individual consultations, including the medication prescribed, and automatically export it to a database held by the PPA (Prescription Pricing Authority) for analysis. Although it was stated that both the patient and prescriber would be anonymised at the practice level, anonymising the prescriber would seem to defeat the purpose, and with this amount of detail, anonymising the patient impossible. I am not clear whether the Information Commissioner was consulted before the project was developed.

I have less confidence in the consistent high quality of GP records – whether or not electronic: some of my patients would probably be found to have Fucibet prescribed for Ischaemic Heart Disease!

I am not clear who, in this Brave New World of Clinical Governance, Appraisal and Reaccredidation, will have access to data for these purposes – or what degree of either anonymisation or patient consent will be in operation.

I am also not clear what happens to data extracted for one purpose and then used for another.

In the case of Cancer Registers – which have no anonymisation whatsoever – the whole database is handed to the National Office of Statistics: could this happen to confidential information of other patients when it is extracted for use within the NHS for patient care – and NHS statistics?

Legal changes

As a GP, in a position of confidence, I have, I believe, a common law and professional duty to preserve my patient's confidentiality.

9.   PRIMIS – Primary Care Information System.

This duty has always been over-ridden in certain specific circumstances – by order of the court and where demanded by statute (e.g. a Notification of Infectious Disease) and a grey area concerned with prevention of crime and protection of vulnerable individuals especially children.

Over the past few years, there has been a mass of legislation, some directly related to medicine and the NHS, and some with wider implications which may impinge on my duties and obligations – or may not... leaving me confused and concerned.

One of my main concerns is the apparently contradictory requirements of the various Acts – and the lack of clarity about how they might affect me and my patients. I am not alone in my concerns, but the legal opinion appears to be that it will take a few test cases to establish how the various statutes apply. I would prefer not to be one of them.

Take, for instance, the Crime and Disorder Act 1998, and the Anti Terrorism Crime and Security Act 2001. The first gives the right to require information in the case of serious crime on the authority of a Chief Constable or Superintendent – and the later extends this to all police forces throughout the world and to suspected serious crime – not simply terrorism and not actual crime, as far as I can see.

How does this tie in with the Human Rights Act and the requirements of the Data Protection Act 1998?

Is it, in fact, against the European Convention of Human Rights, and if so, which takes precedence – or am I potentially equally guilty if I do comply and if I refuse – but under different legislation? Would I have a defence that this catch 22 situation might infringe *my* human rights, possibly under a different clause?

How about my suppliers?

Under regulations under section 60 of the Health and Social Care Act 2001, I might be obliged to provide information regarding whole classes of patients, for example cancer patients. I do not know whether this would be specific items of information, or whether it would be the total medical record. I do know that the whole of this identifiable patient information is then passed to the NOS (National Office of Statistics), but again, I do not know what obligation the NOS has to preserve the individual medical privacy of my individual patient. Using a universal identifier, such as the NHS number, doesn't provide any protection.

Suppose I refused to co-operate – and accepted the £5000 fine this entailed: could my provider be forced to extract the data, with or without my consent? I appreciate they would not do so willingly...

Could the Regulation of Investigatory Powers Act be invoked? Some of the clauses in R.I.P.A are so arcane that *no-one* seems to have much idea as to how they apply, to what and to whom – or their relationship with other legislation and common law. Yet again, much of the impact would appear to depend on regulations under clause 3 (I think), but one of the interesting points is that a section 12 order would prevent the recipient from telling anyone else that they were being investigated... could this be invoked to get at my patient's confidential medical data without my knowing?

I may well be having unwarranted nightmares – but I am not the only GP with similar concerns.

Practical ideas

I hate being totally negative, so I thought I would contribute a possible way forward, as regards the sharing of individual patient information.

This came out of discussions I have had over the years with my patients – an articulate and often opinionated bunch!

On the one hand, they all want total confidentiality – apart from when they have agreed to release information – e.g. life insurance applications – or given implied consent e.g. in connection with a referral.

On the other hand, they think it is insane if my staff cannot say they are diabetics on insulin and allergic to penicillin if they end up in coma in Brighton.

Our joint solution was a minimum data set which would be reasonably freely available – an agreed list of data items, where the receptionist would not be fired if it turned out not to be the SHO in Brighton....

This would also benefit the SHO: in an emergency, would you want to have to read through the Lloyd George envelope, knowing that it was possible something important was missing from the summary?

I am hoping this book will give me guidance as to my legal and practical position – and provide a basis for any decisions I have to make on the professional and ethical issues involved. I really don't want to be either struck off *or* a test case!

Further Reading

Patient Confidentiality and Caldicott Guardians
http://www.doh.gov.uk/nhsexipu/confiden/

Caldicott Report
http://www.doh.gov.uk/confiden/crep.htm

NHS, Strategy and NHSIA
Service with Ambition
http://www.doh.gov.uk

The NHS Plan
http://www.nhs.uk/nhsplan

Building the Information Core – Implementing the NHS Plan
Jan 2001
http://www.doh.gov.uk/nhsexipu/strategy/overview

Statutes
Acts of the UK Parliament and Statutory Instruments quoted in
this book can be accessed through:
http://www.legislation.hmso.gov.uk/legislation/lexhome-content.htm

Other Items of Interest
BMA and Patient Confidentiality – 1995 Paper prepared for the
BMA by Ross Anderson
http://www.cl.cam.ac.uk/users/rja14/bmaupdate/bmaupdate.html

Paperless Practice – guidelines for the paperless practice
http://www.doh.gov.uk/gpepr/guidelines.pdf

PRIMIS
http://www.primis.nottingham.ac.uk/

APPENDICES

APPENDIX 1
HEALTH & SOCIAL CARE ACT 2001

Health and Social Care Act 2001[1]

PART 5

MISCELLANEOUS AND SUPPLEMENTARY

Patient information

60 Control of patient information

(1) The Secretary of State may by regulations make such provision for and in connection with requiring or regulating the processing of prescribed patient information for medical purposes as he considers necessary or expedient–

(a) in the interests of improving patient care, or

(b) in the public interest.

This subsection and subsection (2) have effect subject to subsections (3) to (6).

(2) Regulations under subsection (1) may, in particular, make provision–

(a) for requiring prescribed communications of any nature which contain patient information to be disclosed by health service bodies in prescribed circumstances–

(i) to the person to whom the information relates,

(ii) (where it relates to more than one person) to the person to whom it principally relates, or

(iii) to a prescribed person on behalf of any such person as is mentioned in sub-paragraph (i) or (ii),

in such manner as may be prescribed;

(b) for requiring or authorising the disclosure or other processing of prescribed patient information to or by persons of any prescribed description subject to compliance with any prescribed conditions (including conditions requiring prescribed undertakings to be obtained from such persons as to the processing of such information);

(c) for securing that, where prescribed patient information is processed by a person in accordance with the regulations, anything done by him in so processing the information shall be taken to be lawfully done despite any obligation of confidence owed by him in respect of it;

(d) for creating offences punishable on summary conviction by a fine not exceeding level 5 on the standard scale or such other level as is prescribed or for creating other procedures for enforcing any provisions of the regulations.

(3) Regulations under subsection (3) may not make provision requiring the processing of confidential patient information for any purpose if it would be reasonably practicable to achieve that purpose otherwise than pursuant to such regulations, having regard to the cost of and the technology available for achieving that purpose.

(4) Where regulations under subsection (3) make provision requiring the processing of prescribed confidential patient information, then the Secretary of State–

(a) shall, at any time within the period of one month beginning on each anniversary of the making of such regulations, consider whether any such provision could be included in regulations made at that time without contravening subsection (5), and

(b) if he determines that any such provision could not be so included, shall make further regulations varying or revoking the regulations made under subsection (3) to such extent as he considers necessary in order for the regulations to comply with that subsection.

(5) Regulations under subsection (3) may not make provision for requiring the processing of confidential patient information solely or principally for the purpose of determining the care and treatment to be given to particular individuals.

(6) Without prejudice to the operation of provisions made under subsection (4)(c), regulations under this section may not make provision for or in connection with the processing of prescribed patient information in a manner inconsistent with any provision made by or under the Data Protection Act 1998 (c. 29).

(7) Before making any regulations under this section the Secretary of State shall, to such extent as he considers appropriate in the light of the requirements of section 61, consult such bodies appearing to him to represent the interests of those likely to be affected by the regulations as he considers appropriate.

(8) In this section "patient information" means–

   (a) information (however recorded) which relates to the physical or mental health or condition of an individual, to the diagnosis of his condition or to his care or treatment, and

   (b) information (however recorded) which is to any extent derived, directly or indirectly, from such information,

   whether the identity of the individual in question is ascertainable from the information or not.

(9) For the purposes of this section, patient information is "confidential patient information" where–

   (a) the identity of the individual in question is ascertainable–

      (i)   from that information, or

      (ii) from that information and other information which is in the possession of, or is likely to come into the possession of, the person processing that information, and

   (b) that information was obtained or generated by a person who, in the circumstances, owed an obligation of confidence to that individual.

(10) In this section–

   "the health service" has the same meaning as in the 1977 Act;

   "health service body" means any body (including a government department) or person engaged in the provision of the health service that is prescribed, or of a description prescribed, for the purposes of this definition;

   "medical purposes" means the purposes of any of the following–

   (a) preventative medicine, medical diagnosis, medical research, the provision of care and treatment and the management of health and social care services, and

   (b) informing individuals about their physical or mental health or condition, the diagnosis of their condition or their care or treatment;

   "prescribed" means specified in, or determined in accordance with, regulations made by the Secretary of State under this section;

   "processing", in relation to information, means the use, disclosure or obtaining of the information or the doing of such other things in relation to it as may be prescribed for the purposes of this definition.

61 Patient Information Advisory Group

(1) For the purposes of subsections (2) and (3), the Secretary of State shall, as soon as reasonably practicable after the passing of this Act, by

regulations establish a committee to be known as the Patient Information Advisory Group ("the Advisory Group").

(2) Before laying before Parliament a draft of any statutory instrument containing regulations under section 60(1), or making any regulations pursuant to section 60(4)(b), the Secretary of State shall seek and have regard to the views of the Advisory Group on the proposed regulations.

(3) The Secretary of State may seek the views of the Advisory Group on such other matters connected with the processing of patient information or of any information (other than patient information) obtained or generated in the course of the provision of the health service as he considers appropriate.

(4) Regulations under subsection (1) may, in particular, make provision as to–

   (a) the persons or bodies who are to be represented by members of the Advisory Group,

   (b) the terms of appointment of members,

   (c) the proceedings of the Advisory Group, and

   (d) the payment by the Secretary of State of–

      (i) such expenses incurred by the Advisory Group, and

      (ii) such allowances in respect of expenses incurred by members of the Advisory Group,

   as he may determine.

(5) The Secretary of State shall publish, in such manner as he considers appropriate, any views which he receives from the Advisory Group pursuant to subsection (2).

(6) In this section "the health service", "patient information" and "processing" have the same meaning as they have for the purposes of section 60.

APPENDIX 2
THE CALDICOTT COMMITTEE: REPORT ON THE REVIEW OF PATIENT-IDENTIFIABLE INFORMATION – DECEMBER 1997

Summary

For full text see *http://www.doh.gov.uk/confiden/crep.htm.*

Foreword

This Review was commissioned by the Chief Medical Officer of England owing to increasing concern about the ways in which patient information is used in the NHS in England and Wales and the need to ensure that confidentiality is not undermined.

Such concern was largely due to the development of information technology in the service, and its capacity to disseminate information about patients rapidly and extensively.

In 1996 guidance on *"The Protection and Use of Patient Information"* was promulgated. We need to promote awareness of it at all levels in the NHS.

It is a truism that confidentiality is an essential component of the clinical consultation in the provision of health care. The clinical professions have stringent requirements with regard to confidentiality in their codes of ethics.

However, information about patients, not directly associated with their clinical care, underpins the efficient operation of the NHS, and its importance cannot be overstated. Recent outbreaks of Escherichia infection and geographical variation in the prevalence of particular forms of cancer both illustrate how information about disease, suffered by individual patients in particular locations, provides knowledge which contributes not only to their effective treatment, but also potentially to the prevention of further cases occurring.

It is clearly important that confidentiality does not impede the provision of prompt and effective patient care. But at times there is a tension between the needs of the service for patient information and the expectation of patients that information about them will be kept confidential. It is not uncommon for the NHS to have to balance conflicting needs of this kind; this can be done by adhering to explicit and transparent principles of good practice which we have outlined.

Increasing adherence to the principles will reassure patients and those treating them that confidentiality is safeguarded. Such progress should be monitored and appropriately identified, and individuals held to account wherever patient-identifiable data is present in the Service. We believe that the principles outlined here should also be applied to information identifiable to individual patients concerned with their clinical care, and medical research. It is clear that patients expect nothing less.

I should like to thank the members of my Committee, its Working Groups and the secretariat for their contributions to this Review – not easy deliberations but pursued with much commitment and good humour.

Dame Fiona Caldicott

Executive Summary

i)   In the light of the requirements in The Protection and Use of Patient Information and taking into account work undertaken by a joint Department of Health (DH) and British Medical Association (BMA) Working Group which has been considering NHS Information Management and Technology (IM&T) security and confidentiality, the Chief Medical Officer established the Caldicott Committee to review all patient-identifiable information which passes from National Health Service (NHS) organisations in England to other NHS or non-NHS bodies for purposes other than direct care, medical research, or where there is a statutory requirement for information.

ii) The purpose was to ensure that patient identifiable information is only transferred for justified purposes and that only the minimum necessary information is transferred in each case. Where appropriate, the Committee was asked to advise whether action to minimise risks of breach of confidentiality would be desirable.

iii) The work of the Committee was carried out in an open and consultative manner. Written submissions were sought from many organisations to identify existing concerns, and members of the Committee have met with representatives of a number of key bodies. Working groups containing a wide range of health professionals and managers were established to consider related groups of information flows and to take soundings on emerging findings.

iv) Some 86 flows of patient-identifiable information were mapped relating to a wide range of planning, operational or monitoring purposes. Some of these flows were exemplars, representing locally diverse information flows with broadly similar characteristics and purposes.

v)   The Committee was greatly encouraged to discover that, within the context of current policy, all of the flows identified were for justifiable purposes. However, a number of the flows currently use more patient-identifiable information than is required to satisfy their purposes. Also many of the patient-identifiers currently used (eg name and address) could be omitted if a reliable, but suitably controlled, coded identifier could be used to support identification.

vi) It was recognised that some flows of information were likely to be missed and that flows commence, evolve or are discontinued with such frequency that specific recommendations could soon date. Although specific recommendations have been included where appropriate, in general the recommendations reflect this evolving picture by developing a direction of travel, outlining good practice principles and calling for regular reviews of activity within a clear framework of responsibility.

Summary of Recommendations

Recommendation 1: Every dataflow, current or proposed, should be tested against basic principles of good practice. Continuing flows should be re-tested regularly.

Recommendation 2: A programme of work should be established to reinforce awareness of confidentiality and information security requirements amongst all staff within the NHS.

Recommendation 3: A senior person, preferably a health professional, should be nominated in each health organisation to act as a guardian, responsible for safeguarding the confidentiality of patient information.

Recommendation 4: Clear guidance should be provided for those individuals/bodies responsible for approving uses of patient-identifiable information.

Recommendation 5: Protocols should be developed to protect the exchange of patient-identifiable information between NHS and non-NHS bodies.

Recommendation 6: The identity of those responsible for monitoring the sharing and transfer of information within agreed local protocols should be clearly communicated.

Recommendation 7: An accreditation system which recognises those organisations following good practice with respect to confidentiality should be considered.

Recommendation 8: The NHS number should replace other identifiers wherever practicable, taking account of the consequences of errors and particular requirements for other specific identifiers.

Recommendation 9: Strict protocols should define who is authorised to gain access to patient identity where the NHS number or other coded identifier is used.

Recommendation 10: Where particularly sensitive information is transferred, privacy enhancing technologies (e.g. encrypting identifiers or "patient identifying information") must be explored.

Recommendation 11: Those involved in developing health information systems should ensure that best practice principles are incorporated during the design stage.

Recommendation 12: Where practicable, the internal structure and administration of databases holding patient-identifiable information should reflect the principles developed in this report.

Recommendation 13: The NHS number should replace the patient's name on Items of Service Claims made by General Practitioners as soon as practically possible.

Recommendation 14: The design of new systems for the transfer of prescription data should incorporate the principles developed in this report.

Recommendation 15: Future negotiations on pay and conditions for General Practitioners should, where possible, avoid systems of payment which require patient identifying details to be transmitted.

Recommendation 16: Consideration should be given to procedures for General Practice claims and payments which do not require patient-identifying information to be transferred, which can then be piloted.

APPENDIX 3
BUILDING THE INFORMATION CORE
– IMPLEMENTING THE NHS PLAN

1 Summary

1.1 This document considers the implications of the NHS Plan for the necessary information and IT infrastructure that will support the patient centred delivery of care and services. It builds on and updates *Information for Health*, the information strategy for the NHS, and provides a clearer focus on what our priorities for successful delivery need to be. It details what will be delivered over the next few years and the actions required to ensure successful implementation. This document is also supported by more detailed online material which can be found at: *www.doh.gov.uk/ipu/strategy/update/*

1.2 Whilst the *e-government strategic framework* requires "building services around citizens' choices", the NHS Plan requires an "NHS designed around the patient". The *NHS Plan* stresses the need to support well co-ordinated "seamless" services across "whole systems". The information and IT systems needed to deliver these objectives must be capable of being personalised to meet the needs of the individuals who provide these services as well as those who receive them. *Information for Health* sets out a strategic direction that supports both the NHS Plan and e-government. But, whilst much has been achieved in the two years since its launch, much remains to be done and it is time to update it in the light of the new policy agenda and developments in technology.

1.3 The vision of the NHS Plan focuses on a redesigned care system. *Chapter 3* of this document illustrates how information and IT will support the modernisation of NHS organisations that will be delivering preventive care, enabling self-care, and providing primary care, hospital care and intermediate care. It also shows what this might mean from the perspective of the delivery of cancer services. There is much to do in bridging the gap between the NHS now and a service shaped around the needs and preferences of individuals. There is an urgency to put workable and person centred systems and solutions throughout the NHS and enable links with social care. And, in doing this, it is vital that information and IT is used to improve the delivery of good quality services, and to help the NHS get the best out of its investment in its most valuable resource – its staff. Getting best value from the £10bn spent by the NHS each year on goods and services by exploiting the opportunities of e-commerce also requires a properly networked NHS.

1.4   Given the developments in the policy environment, and emergence of an increasing variety of electronic channels over which services can be delivered, what are the requirements of the different stakeholders – and in particular patients and the public, clinicians and managers – across all types of NHS organisation? *Chapter 4* presents these requirements in terms of:

- Information Services (e.g. *NHS Direct, National electronic Library for Health*)

- *Electronic Records* (both within organisations and between them)

- National or Local applications (such as Human Resources and Payroll).

It is access to these sorts of services that helps individuals take better informed decisions. But to deliver them requires a properly developed infrastructure and standards.

1.5   *Chapter 5* makes it clear that in developing the essential infrastructure it is important that standards, once agreed, are used across the NHS. By having a standard infrastructure, new and innovative ideas which can be shown to work can be rolled-out much more quickly and effectively than at present. But the first step is to continue *Project Connect* (connecting GPs to NHSnet) and get all NHS staff connected with "desktop" access to some basic tools. Safe and secure access to the networked NHS for health and social care professionals is essential to this infrastructure, as is the process of making information skills a basic part of the education and training of all staff.

1.6   Putting in place the essential infrastructure that enables services to be delivered electronically to the end-users when and where they want it is a major implementation exercise that needs to be properly supported. *Chapter 6* outlines the key roles of different parts of the NHS organisations, and stresses the importance of developing partnership arrangements. These include working in partnership across local health economies and with IT suppliers. Encouraging innovations and using the outcome of them as one way of improving procurement is important. Developing more national solutions, framework agreements and catalogues to speed up procurements is vital. With appropriate partnerships, the potential to exploit the NHS brand to help develop knowledge resources is considerable.

1.7   Delivering the information core, converting policy into practice, needs clear targets to be set. *Chapter 7* sets out what they are for connecting NHS staff, delivering information, electronic records and national applications, together with local planning and preparation. Building the information core will meet the commitments of the NHS Plan and deliver the right solutions for patients, the public, NHS staff and all care professionals and workers. In short it will deliver:

- by March 2001 – 95% of GP practices and 25% of Trust clinical staff with NHSnet connections and using NHS information services such as the National electronic Library for Health

- by March 2002 – desktop connections for NHS clinical staff to basic e-mail, browsing and directory services, and roll out of NHS cryptography support services begins

- by March 2003 – migration to national standards for e-mail, browsing and office systems completed and all NHS staff with desktop access, and clinical information systems start to use the SNOMED Clinical Terms

- by March 2004 – major national payroll/HR systems implemented

- by 2005 – a vibrant networked NHS, with booking systems in place, electronic transfer of records within primary care, all acute Trusts with level 3 Electronic Patient Records and first generation Electronic Health Records.

2 The Case for Change

- **What has been achieved so far?**

2.1   *To deliver the NHS Plan,* information and IT must be an intrinsic part of the agenda for change. The principles, objectives and direction of travel set by the national information strategy in September 1998 remain. However much of the reform and innovation necessary to translate the NHS Plan into practice requires a hard look at information management and how to make the best use of modern information and communication technologies in healthcare. The challenge is to enable the patient centred delivery of care and services by delivering an appropriate information infrastructure.

2.2   People across society are rapidly changing the way they live, work and play through the application of and interaction with modern information and communication technologies. The e-government *"strategic framework for public services in the Information Age"* and the associated targets for delivering public services in new and electronic ways aim to ensure that public services are an integral part of this radical transformation of our society. The challenge is to innovate and in particular to: *"improve public services for the benefits of citizens: to be more convenient, more joined-up, more responsive and more personalised"* (e-gov: Electronic Government Services for the 21st Century September 2000).

2.3   The NHS Plan will give people a health service fit for the 21st Century by shaping its services around the needs and preferences of patients. *"Step by step over the next ten years the NHS must be redesigned to be patient centred – to offer a personalised service"* (NHS Plan July 2000). Over the next few years individuals will have far greater information about how they can look after

their own health and how they can use their local services. They will have the
option of having much more information about the care being planned for
them and the possible outcomes. Waiting for their tests, diagnosis or any
stage of treatment will be reduced. They will have the right to see their own
medical records and will require easier access to records. They will be able to
book their own appointments and have better out-of-hours services.

What has been achieved so far?		
Commitment	**Achievement**	**Benefits**
To ensure the NHS copes with the Year 2000 problem	The NHS was fully prepared for the date change. As a result of good planning there was no adverse effect of patient services, staff or safety	Considerable investment in IT infrastructure updated and improved NHS systems
NHS Direct services to cover England by end of October 2000	NHS Direct now covers the whole population of England with almost 50,000 calls per week handled through 22 call centres	Provides 24 hour access to advice, information and care services and has already transformed many peoples experience of the NHS
To improve public access to information on healthcare and services	*NHS Direct Online* is receiving 1 million hits per week from over 17,500 visitor sessions	Provides trustworthy and clearly branded advice and information on keeping healthy, self-care and illnesses and treatments. Enables the patient to be an informed partner in their own care
To improve access to knowledge bases and evidence based information	The full pilot *National electronic Library for Health* was launched in November 2000	Provides online knowledge and know-how through new resources such as Clinical Evidence and makes the Cochrane Library available to the whole NHS
All computerised GP practices to be connected to NHSnet by March 2002	80% of computerised GP practices are connected to NHSnet along with all health authorities and 95% of NHS trusts by December 2000	Increasing potential for desk top access to e-mail and web browsing, with in built capability to support messaging and booking

What has been achieved so far?		
Commitment	**Achievement**	**Benefits**
To *review the cost and benefits* of the time spent on collecting data for Koerner returns	The instructions to stop recording total face to face contacts on a number of central returns has been issued	Less time will be spent by care professionals collecting information and the NHS can decide locally to adopt more appropriate measures of performance and delivery in community services
To support patient care through *electronic records*	Four health communities are piloting electronic health records to share patient information across health and social care. A further 13 NHS sites are focusing on the delivery of patient care in a range of settings, from NHS Direct to mental health or cancer care	A person's health record will be available at the time they are seen and will hold a complete and up to date summary of their clinical history or current condition. This work is essential to developing national standards for electronic records
To remove the contractual requirement for GPs to maintain paper records	From October 2000 the terms of service for GPs have been amended to allow them to maintain all or part of their patient records on a computer system	GPs can now provide the full benefits of running paperless practice
To develop pathology messaging for exchanging electronic results	The first Trust systems pathology EDI specification including an updated GP specification has been published	NHS wide and electronic pathology results and messaging will reduce delays in treatment, potential errors in paper based reports and provide cost savings
Improve funding for IT investment	In the last two years to March 2001 additional funding for IT has totalled £214m.	The NHS will have spent over £1.5 billion on IM&T in the three years to March 2001. The Departmental Investment Strategy published in November 2000 sets out the intention to invest an additional £851m to March 2004 over and above annual NHS spend

What has been achieved so far?		
Commitment	Achievement	Benefits
Develop Local Implementation Strategies for information and IT	There are 98 LISs providing clear and costed plans for working through the original goals in *Information for Health*	Local partnership and planning provides real confidence in the ability of health communities to satisfy their information and IT needs and deliver national priorities

2.4 Despite such good and positive progress the NHS Plan highlighted certain home truths about the use of information and IT in the delivery of care and services. *"Information is not shared and investigations are often repeated. Delay seems designed into the system." "Performance has been inhibited by lack of reliable information for clinicians, managers and patients." "The NHS needs a system which spots problems early on, takes action swiftly and can act decisively." "The NHS has inadequate levels of modern equipment. IT investment has been too slow and too patchy."*

2.5 This reinforces the need to deliver the key objectives and targets from the information strategy and put in place the information core and infrastructure outlined in this overview. Through urgent and co-ordinated action we will address such shortcomings and ensure that we achieve real benefits for patients and the public, and lasting improvements to the service provided.

3 Supporting a Service Designed around the Individual: the Role of Information and IT

- **Preventive care**

- **Intermediate care**

- **Self-care**

- **Quality of care**

- **Primary care**

- **Investing in NHS staff**

- **Hospital care**

- **e-commerce**

3.1 The vision of the NHS Plan focuses on a redesigned care system. Bridging the gap between the NHS now and the vision of fast and convenient care delivered to a consistently high standard requires a greater sense of urgency in delivering visible and workable information and IT solutions. Introducing information systems and the electronic delivery of services has to be understood as a business, not a technological, issue. We must not lose sight of the fact that the purpose of improving the use of information and IT is to ensure that people receive the best possible care, and through making quality outcome data available we will monitor the continuing effectiveness of that care. The key lies in integrating information across the various parts of health and social care to achieve a single or "whole" system centred around the individual that also meets the requirements of all parts of the care system e.g. primary Care Trusts, NHS walk-in centres or NHS Direct. In this context we need to explain the role and benefits of improving the quality and management of information and harnessing modern technology alongside the model of care given in the NHS Plan. Examples are provided to show how the information infrastructure required by the Plan will impact on the delivery of cancer services.

Preventive care

3.2   Information systems will help care professionals deliver preventive care by supporting health promotion advice and screening services. They provide decision support and alerting systems to prompt the provision of advice during the consultation, or provide customised advice on paper, or prompt referral to advice and support groups. In addition, they will facilitate the development of routine call and recall systems through disease and patient group registers as well as supporting the major screening programmes. The information strategies to support National Service Framework topics are an initial focus for this work.

3.3   NHS Direct will also be taking a more proactive role in helping people manage their medicines, get the most out of a course of treatment or check that the more vulnerable people are better targeted with direct advice and support. Because the most vulnerable are also the least likely to have computers, mobile phones or digital TV, improvements must also be made to the information networks that support alternative and familiar services e.g. the telephone, community facilities or face to face contact. For example, Lincolnshire Health Authority in collaboration with the Local Authority provides free community wide access to NHS Direct Online. This includes a free printed copy of any information required in all 46 public libraries, numerous local pharmacies and shops, several GP practices' waiting areas and the reception area of Pilgrim Hospital, Boston. Some 60% of users of this service are aged over 60.

Implications for Cancer Services

The Smith family routinely use the Internet for online banking, income tax returns, booking travel and holidays, reading the OFSTED reports on their children's schools or to supplement their children's studies. They expect to access information on health and healthcare in the same way. They also expect the health professionals they visit to use information systems to provide accurate, tailored and timely health promotion and healthcare advice.

Mrs Smith has a family history of breast cancer and looks to her GP and local specialist services to offer the best advice and monitor her health through the development of population and disease topic registers. Mrs Smith also regularly visits NHS Direct Online for accredited information on reducing the risk of developing cancer through a healthier diet and for public versions of evidence-based guidance on prevention and treatment breakthroughs. She maintains a personalised online health record that amongst other things provides a risk score based in part on her family's history of cancer.

Self-care

3.4   People deal with some 80% of healthcare episodes through self-care. If the frontline in healthcare is the home then easy access to the right advice, information and services has to be made available from the home. All care providers must consider what it means to be a remote resource which people can use routinely every day to help look after themselves and their families and how they need to support such use.

3.5   People will be helped to navigate the maze of health and care information through the development of consistent information and services with easy access from the home or key public places close to home. Providing good quality and trustworthy content is well under way. NHS Direct Online provides information on healthy living, self help, illnesses, conditions, treatments and outcomes and will soon feature information on local care and services and how best to use them. A further step is to group information and services around common events or *life episodes*, e.g. "having a baby", to result in better co-ordinated and more meaningful information for the citizen with better access to the full range of relevant public services: health, social security, housing etc. This citizen-focused approach is central to the e-government strategy.

Implications for Cancer Services

More, and more accessible, information to help people like Mrs Smith recognise the signs and symptoms of cancer is available through the Internet, digital TV health channels, public information kiosks, GP surgeries, NHS walk-in centres, libraries and advice centres e.g. Citizen Advice Bureau. It is important that Mrs Smith is "breast aware" and reports any changes to her GP. Her GP can refer a woman of any age for consultation and assessment if he or she feels that this is clinically necessary.

Primary care

3.6   At the moment some 90% of patient contacts with the NHS are through primary care. We need to build on the strengths of co-ordination and continuity of care provided by primary care and to support GPs and primary care teams in delivering more patient centred services. The creation of new Care Trusts will bring about even closer integration of health and social services which, together with the extension of Personal Medical Services and NHS walk-in centres, will allow more flexible primary care services to evolve.

3.7   Recognising the need to provide better and more convenient services to individuals, the NHS Plan sets out ambitious targets to provide comprehensive systems for booked appointments by 2005. GPs or practice staff will be able to book their patients into outpatient clinics at hospitals, and within hospitals patients will also be given booked appointments for inpatient or daycase care. In due course making booked appointments with other health and social care providers will become routine.

3.8   In addition, the new one-stop primary care centres including GPs and other members of the Primary Health Care Team working alongside dentists, opticians, pharmacists and social care workers will provide faster more accessible services to people. The new interface between health and social care provision has significant business implications in developing joint patient assessment, monitoring and review systems. These new services will need to be supported by modernised primary care information systems capable of improving the co-ordination of services between different professionals and agencies involved with individuals leading to an improved quality of care. These same systems are also needed to support the implementation of National Service Frameworks, ensuring older people receive a one-stop service, providing repeat dispensing schemes to make obtaining repeat prescriptions easier for patients with chronic conditions, providing integrated care pathways or for clinical audit and Clinical Governance.

3.9   Providing care professionals with access to common and consistent decision support systems will ensure that they are able to offer people the best diagnosis, referral and care across the country, translating research evidence and best practice into day-to-day practice. Access to such common evidence-based decision support systems – provided across a common national technical infrastructure – will enable consistently high standards of care to be provided, regardless of the setting – e.g. in A&E departments, NHS walk-in centres or NHS Direct call centres.

3.10 The 36 *NHS walk-in centre* pilots being set up across England will provide a complementary service to GP surgeries and A&E departments by offering a service at convenient times. They are particularly suited to those people who find it difficult to get an appointment with their GP or attend A&E departments with a minor problem. Using the same decision support software as NHS Direct centres, walk-in centres will be able to assess and treat patients with minor illnesses and injuries, referring on where it is appropriate to do so. They work closely with local health and social care providers to provide a holistic package of care. Using Patient Group Directions, walk-in centre nurses will be able to supply medicines for common ailments and conditions. New information systems will ensure that continuity of care is not jeopardised by ensuring that – subject to patient consent – information about walk-in centre contacts flows through to the patients' GPs.

3.11 NHS Direct will provide a one stop gateway to care to give people more choice about accessing the NHS, accessing out-of-hours care or receiving treatment without visiting the GP practice. NHS Direct nurses will advise on care at home, visiting the local pharmacist, making a routine appointment, arranging for an emergency consultation, calling an ambulance or getting social services support. New information systems and networks are the practical means to more closely integrate NHS Direct and existing health and social care services. The new Care Direct service aims to improve access to, and information about, services for older people and disabled people who have no prospect of work.

3.12 The GP practice will become the place where:

- appointments for consultations or operations can be booked directly – giving patients more choice and convenience, with less wasted time through cancelled appointments and improved management of waiting lists

- more diagnosis is carried out using video and tele-links to hospital based specialists – giving patients more equitable access to care, less waiting and travelling and clinicians more appropriate referrals, improved use of resources and better continuing professional development

- test results are ordered and received electronically – giving patients less delay and worry and clinicians less bureaucracy with earlier diagnosis and treatment and improved outcomes.

3.13   *Information for Health* set key targets for modernising primary care information systems that have now been augmented by additional targets up to 2004 in the NHS Plan. These include:

- the majority of NHS staff to be working in accordance with protocols for all common conditions

- a major increase in GPs working to PMS contracts tied to quality targets

- access by patients to Electronic Patient Records

- 50% of primary and community trusts to have Electronic Patient Record systems

- ensuring that Care Trusts have the information systems necessary to support the delivery of integrated health and social care services.

Implications for Cancer Services

Following Mrs Smith's routine attendance for breast screening she was diagnosed with breast cancer. When she saw the consultant, the consultant went through the NICE guidelines on breast cancer and cancer drugs with Mrs Smith before printing out copies and a summary of the consultation for her to take home. The following day Mrs Smith realised there were more questions she would like answered and made an appointment to see her GP, Dr Brown. Dr Brown was able to call up Mrs Smith's medical history, test results and notes from the consultation at the cancer unit. Mrs Smith had been advised to have surgery and armed with the full facts and the same NICE guidelines, Dr Brown was able to answer all outstanding questions. The GP was also able to call up reassuring survival data for women with the same early stage of breast cancer and performance information to show that the local cancer unit had better than the national average results.

Hospital care

3.14   Changes similar to those outlined above apply equally to hospitals. On the spot booking systems do not just make a hospital appointment more convenient for patients, they also act as a driver for more fundamental reform. There is still a significant challenge facing NHS Trusts to implement the Electronic Patient Record targets that form the centrepiece of *Information for Health*.

3.15   Co-ordinated local investment in new systems for booking, automated scheduling, patient administration, electronic records, ordering tests and results (pathology and radiology) or electronic prescribing will bring modern information and communication technology to all staff, from reception through A&E, X-ray or blood tests to clinics and consultations. In the clinics or on the wards the aim is to enable doctors and nurses to request an X-ray or blood test at their desks or at the bedside, receive back the time and date for the investigation, perhaps with a timed portering request registered at the same time. The patients will see that activity and information centres on them and have the confidence that the doctors, nurses and departments have access to the right information at the right time.

Implications for Cancer Services

Mrs Smith was confident that she received the best information, support and specialist care to help her and her family cope with cancer, from the time the test revealed an abnormality throughout the subsequent stages of the disease and treatment. Good communication between her and the care professionals was an essential feature of her experience.

Behind the scenes NHSnet linked all organisations providing primary, hospital and intermediate care. Tried and tested information sharing protocols were used by health and social care professionals, and multi-agency care pathways were supported by modern information systems. Mrs Smith was given the best possible chance of a complete cure because her cancer was identified at a very early stage of development and because she received urgent referral and treatment. Her patient experience was improved through pre-scheduled diagnostic investigations, pre-booked appointments, multi-disciplinary working and the delivery of appropriate treatment.

Intermediate care

3.16   People want to get on with their lives with the minimum of disruption from illness, injury or disability. Information and communication technology offers critical support to a new range of intermediate services that will provide a bridge between hospital and home and deliver as much service as possible in or close to the convenience of the person's home.

3.17   Seamless care for individuals and an underpinning care and discharge plan hinges on easy access to electronic records and care plans. There must be the capacity to *share information across health and social care* and amongst rapid response or hospital-at-home teams that need to work on an integrated basis with GPs, community nurses, physiotherapists and social care staff.

3.18   Telecare and telemonitoring is already making independent living possible in a working pilot for older people in sheltered housing in Tyneside. Other pilots in home distance monitoring of patients with high blood pressure demonstrate enhanced efficiency, improved outcomes and the more active involvement of individuals in their own care.

3.19   Figure 1 is a generalised map of a patient pathway, with appropriate access and pre-booked treatment plans. It is generally applicable to any patient with cancer or any non-cancer patient. Co-ordinating the patient journey is critical and the ability to electronically refer a patient into the system, electronically book the patient from one landmark to the next and electronically chart the patient's progress is a logical progression of the co-ordination process. Healthcare professionals will be able to quickly access information about previous contacts, regardless of whether they are working in general practice, specialist cancer units or in the community. Ensuring that there are appropriate data sets for each point on the patient journey will form an important element of the Electronic Patient Record.

Figure 1 – A Patient Pathway

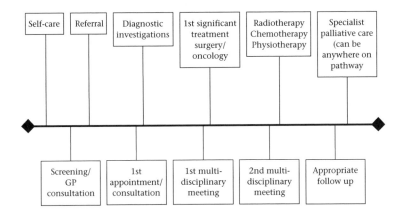

Quality of care

3.20   The NHS Plan sets out the main national priorities. Individuals should have fair access and high standards of care wherever they live. It confirms the importance of the quality framework laid out in *"A First Class Service"*.

Figure 2 – The Quality Framework

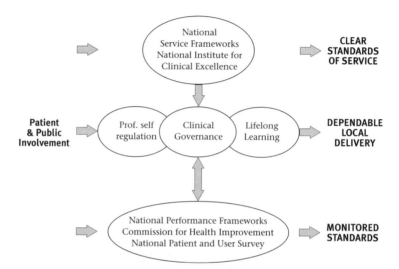

What the Quality Framework means for Patients

3.21   At a national level the Department of Health will, with the help of leading clinicians, managers and staff, set national standards in the priority areas. The national standards for key conditions and diseases will be set through *National Service Frameworks* (NSFs) and the *National Institute for Clinical Excellence* (NICE). NSFs have already been produced covering mental health and coronary heart disease. The country's first ever comprehensive *National Cancer Plan* was published in September 2000. An NSF for older people's services will be published later this winter and for diabetes in 2001. These five frameworks between them cover around half of the total NHS spending. In addition, the *NSF information strategy programme* is developing information strategies to support cancer and other clinical priority areas discussed in the NHS Plan. The *Cancer Information Strategy* was published in June 2000 and the Mental Health Information Strategy should be available in January 2001. Information strategies to support coronary heart disease, care of older people and diabetes are now in preparation.

3.22   Putting in place the information systems that support National Service Frameworks will assist the delivery of individual care and, by adding information about outcomes, will provide the basis for the routine systematic collection of person-based data to populate indicators of clinical performance, support *Clinical Governance* and performance management. Coupled with information about populations, this data can also be used to better target resources to address inequalities of health and healthcare service provision.

3.23   *Information for Health* is an essential part of the quality programme. The modern information systems being put in place will support the NHS and partner agencies in improving care delivery, accessing agreed protocols and guidance, auditing clinical and practice performance against standards and benchmarks, and in reviewing performance through the *Performance Assessment Framework*. In addition to supporting the delivery of better care by improving the individual's journey through care services, person-based and integrated information systems will support improvement in the quality of care by:

- providing clinical guidelines from NICE, other national and local protocols and guidance and care pathways at the point of care

- reducing the possibility of error through, for example, providing doctors and nurses with easy access to agreed care protocols

- supporting clinicians undertaking appraisal and Clinical Governance

- producing performance management and planning information as a by-product of the information required to support care delivery and linking through to Local Authority data to support the production of Health Improvement Programmes, community plans or local strategic partnerships.

Implications for Cancer Services

The main benefits for cancer patients and their carers from supporting the delivery of high quality services with information are:

- more consistent treatment as health and other care professionals provide care on the basis of national guidance

- protocols and care pathways are available to patients, carers and health and other professionals at the point of care

- a reduction in errors as the lessons learned from adverse incidents are incorporated into information systems and clinical teams alerted to, for example, drug reactions

- care by multi-disciplinary teams whose members are supported in the continuous review of the quality of the care they provide through the provision of clinical audit data (as a by-product of the data they collect to provide care) for appraisal and Clinical Governance purposes,

- services which are commissioned and planned on the basis of need

- the availability of information about how services compare with each other.

Investing in NHS staff

3.24   The NHS plan recognises the value of staff in three main ways:

- the NHS needs more staff – crucially healthcare professionals

- staff need up to date competencies and skills

- NHS organisations need to recognise and reward their contributions in tangible ways

3.25   This has significant implications for both the information needed and the operational systems support – for streamlining recruitment, facilitating more flexible working and for ensuring that the right resources to deliver care are available when and where needed.

3.26   There is a major behavioural, culture change and organisational development challenge in redesigning care services around the individual, and establishing a "network NHS". Everyone – individuals, multi-disciplinary teams and care organisations – will need to think through the way that they work. Information is central to the process of redesigning care systems centred around the individual. Ensuring the quality of care involves being able to identify areas of weakness for individuals and teams, and to access and complete appropriate learning programmes.

3.27   New technologies will not only support clinical practice and care management but also the actual education and training process through the development of knowledge management and e-learning capabilities. New Human Resource systems will develop personal learning records and an integral training management system to ensure progress towards continuous performance improvement for all staff. They will track when improvements are shown to be needed, and support the linkage of personal development plans and training to the delivery of the best possible care. Better HR information will also support workforce planning and help to get the numbers of new healthcare professionals in training right. Medical schools and training places for healthcare professionals will need to be supported by better access to shared e-learning resources. Paragraphs 5.13 to 5.18 provide further details about the implications for the education and training of staff.

3.28   The National electronic Library for Health (NeLH) is being established as an authoritative source of current healthcare knowledge to improve clinical practice and enable the most appropriate treatment to be provided based on accredited clinical evidence. NeLH will complement existing library and information services and offer an increasing range of e-resources and skills to support their use.

e-commerce

3.29   Organisations throughout the world are exploiting the new wave of opportunities presented by e-commerce to revolutionise their own activities, and their interactions with their supplier base. Such opportunities exist for the NHS and its extensive supplier base, covering potentially almost £10 billion of NHS revenue spent each year on goods and services. Exploiting the benefits of e-commerce is a key part of e-government and the *NHS Purchasing and Supply Agency* is currently undertaking research and development work to provide a strategic framework for e-commerce in the NHS. The aim is to realise benefits not only from improving processes and greater purchasing leverage, but also from consolidating, making more transparent, and exploiting, information throughout the supply networks that serve the NHS.

4   Delivering Information

- **How will information and IT fit together?**

- **Information services**

- **Electronic records**

- **National/Local applications**

How will information and IT fit together?

4.1   There are many ways in which information and IT can be used to support the implementation of the NHS Plan. Figure 3 presents a generic model developed to illustrate the translation between policy and practice and how different types of users can access the information they need to make decisions. They can do this through a variety of electronic media or delivery channels. But access to information services, records and applications that are of good quality has to be supported by the development of a national infrastructure and appropriate standards. To support the implementation of the infrastructure and services, there are some important enabling and management issues to be addressed.

Figure 3 – The Information Core

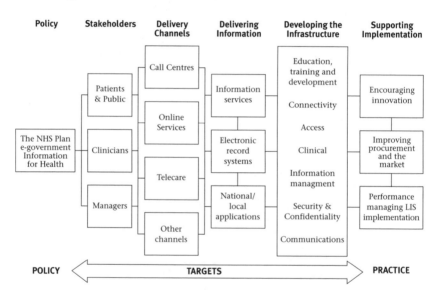

4.2   The NHS Plan and e-government require information, applications and services to be delivered in new ways and through modern systems. The key to such change lies in full workplace access to information, electronic records and a variety of other applications wherever this is required – on the desktop, in the surgery, in the outpatients clinic, at the bedside and on the move. This in turn relies on secure and robust electronic media to facilitate:

- the rapid and safe sharing of information

- access to individual patient and client records for emergency care

- access to the latest knowledge, evidence-base and clinical guidelines for improved decision making and professional development

- the improved use of up-to-date and high quality aggregate information in managing and monitoring performance and planning future services

- modern and streamlined procedures for all staff, to ensure better services to individuals and to increase the internal efficiency of care organisations

- faster communications with colleagues and patients.

Information services

4.3   The NHS must be a major provider of information services in support of care services, working with carefully selected partners to provide a range of information to patients, clinicians and others. It must embrace multi-channel communications and ensure that the strength of a revitalised NHS brand is recognised not only nationally but also internationally. Patients and the public will demand far greater information about how they can look after their own health and about their local services. NHS Direct Online, with information on healthy living and personal healthcare, is currently receiving up to 1 million hits a week from over 17,500 visitor sessions. The public and NHS staff will be able to access information on local care services and how best to use them through nhs.uk and evidence-based information and clinical guidelines through the National electronic Library for Health (NeLH).

NHS Direct Online – comprehensive online information on healthy living, illnesses, conditions and treatments with interactive healthcare guide and monthly feature. October featured depression and in a key collaboration with the Centre for Evidence Based Mental Health at Oxford University they presented the first ever guide to depression, interactive tools for recognising the symptoms, evidence based treatment summaries and audio/video material. 'Find your local pharmacist' online service available from 18 December 2000 to help people requiring out of hours or Christmas holiday services. Information on dentists and opticians to be published by April 2001. Proposals are being developed for email enquiry service to improve interactivity and responsiveness.

NHS Direct Information Points – 150 touch screen information points are now in place, providing public access to the information provided on NHS Direct Online. Over 500 information points will be in place by 2004.

nhs.uk – initial NHS organisational directory in place. Robust technical infrastructure and bandwidth also in place that easily coped with 8,000 hits in one hour when NHS Plan published. News section, Chief Executive briefing service and "Your Guide to the NHS" for patients (replacing the Patients' Charter) to be live in early 2001. Online public information on local healthcare services, healthcare priorities and performance to be published by April 2001.

NeLH – launched pilot core service in November to include evidence-based sources (Cochrane, Clinical Evidence and Bandolier) with links to other quality resources (BNF, electronic library for social care and NHS Direct Online). A key service will provide the research evidence behind the health news stories. Specialised web sites – Virtual Branch Libraries – will focus on mental health, cancer and primary care. The pilot will also test usage and access management services.

NHS Digital – a programme of pilot projects will explore the potential of digital TV in health and test a range of relevant applications. The new television technology opens up new possibilities for rapid access to health advice and information to enhance NHS Direct services, for supporting patient groups, such as those concerned with chronic conditions and for targeting health promotion initiatives to schools or the workplace.

Electronic records

4.4   Wherever a patient is treated, there is a record of that treatment. These are "organisational records" and at present they are, in the main, paper records. New technology gives us opportunities for making those records safer and available for other health professionals. These organisational records will become the Electronic Patient Records (EPRs), and a subset of them will contribute to a lifelong record of a patient's health and healthcare – the Electronic Health Record (EHR).

4.5   Electronic records are crucial to the full development of a patient centred service. They are a major step forward in delivering the type of service people expect from a modern NHS and ensure that:

   •   patients have access to reliable information to improve their knowledge and involvement in their own treatment and care

   •   healthcare professionals have routine and rapid access to relevant clinical guidelines, evidence-base and an individual's medical history and current condition to enable them to provide the highest quality care when and where it is needed

   •   health managers and planners have ready access to aggregate information to improve analysis and decision-making.

4.6   The original *Information for Health* targets for full Electronic Patient Records and an Electronic Health Record for use in 24-hour emergency care by March 2005 remain unchanged. However, with the new requirement for electronic appointment booking and specific requirement to provide personal access to electronic records more quickly than was envisaged in 1998, we are improving the support to help achieve these targets and added applications. By March 2001 the National Patient Access Team will publish a national Strategic Outline Case setting out the preferred approach for implementing electronic booking systems up to 2005.

4.7   From October 2000 a change was made to the General Practitioner's terms of service to legitimise the use of Electronic Patient Records in general practice. There will be national guidance on integrating primary and community EPRs and their architecture and content by September 2001, along with a national approach for implementing the emergency care Electronic Health Record following an assessment of the interim outcomes from current pilots in NHS sites. The use of a modern set of clinical terms underpins many aspects of the development of health information systems. Such a set must meet the needs of all clinical professionals in both primary and secondary care. The development of SNOMED® Clinical Terms is being vigorously supported to achieve this, together with a programme of testing to ensure it can be implemented.

4.8   The NHS Plan referred to the opportunity to provide smart cards for patients to allow easier access to health records. The technical study to consider the potential applications of smart cards and the likely costs and benefits has been completed. A separate study, to examine the wider cultural issues associated with the use of smart cards, is due to be completed in March 2001. Together the results of these studies will inform our future policy on the development of smart card technology in healthcare.

> Up to 2002 the national electronic record development and implementation programme is exploring a number of issues associated with the collection, and sharing of electronic records, including the provision of patient access to information.
>
> In June 2001 the work of the demonstrator sites will be assessed with a view to making policy statements by September 2001 in areas such as the development of the 24 hour emergency EHR, standards for primary/community EPRs etc.
>
> Subject to successful development and testing for implementability, after 1 April 2003 any computerised information system being developed to support any clinical information system, such as EPRs and EHRs, should use the NHS preferred clinical terminology, *SNOMED® Clinical Terms*. Users/suppliers are advised not to develop new Read Code based systems from April 2003.
>
> The role of the patient held smart card in providing access to health records will be the subject of two short studies due to report by March 2001.

National/Local applications

4.9   National and local applications must focus on turning policy potential into operational practice. They are as much about developing national systems, e.g. manpower and payroll systems, as embedding national applications in local systems – e.g. PRODIGY for decision support to improve prescribing. The NHS Wide Clearing Service provides the opportunity to deliver national dataflows to support the information requirements of the Performance Assessment Framework, and to minimise the need for separate dataflows. The key is to ensure developments are made and tested at the appropriate level with the lessons, results and benefits shared by everyone.

4.10   We have a key project underway to procure and implement a new national payroll and human resources system across the whole NHS. This will give the NHS enhanced HR functionality, integrated with the payroll. This will provide support for improved workforce planning, recruitment, better rostering and more flexible working, personal and professional development, and staff performance management.

4.11 The aim is to provide the NHS with a powerful and flexible system that will underpin the new staff-focused initiatives such as the Human Resource Performance Framework. It will reduce the current fragmentation of systems by delivering a single common solution to cover the NHS in England, and is an example of the more standardised approach that we wish to pursue.

> All NHS Direct sites and NHS walk-in centres will be using the NHS Clinical Assessment Systems by summer 2001.
>
> *NHS Strategic Tracing Service* is now live; online tracing is being implemented and will be available across the country by March 2001.
>
> A contract for the national integrated Human Resources and Payroll system will be awarded in 2001.

5   Developing the Essential Infrastructure

- **Setting standards**

- **Getting connected**

- **Ensuring security and confidentiality**

- **Education and training**

5.1 The delivery of applications and knowledge, wherever these are required, depends on a robust and reliable information and IT infrastructure. We have already made good progress, but the objectives of the NHS Plan, the aims of delivering electronic services to the public and technological advances highlight the need for an infrastructure which is robust, flexible, secure and standardised.

Setting Standards

5.2 In line with the NHS Plan, and in response to feedback from the NHS and the supplier community, we are introducing a far more robust approach to standardisation. An infrastructure based on universal Internet technology, government-wide standards and those developed specifically to meet the needs of the NHS will give all staff the means to access the right information in the right place at the right time.

5.3 This cannot happen by chance. We have set up an *NHS Information Standards Board*, responsible for agreeing the standards to be used. Three sub-groups will address clinical information standards, standards for management information and a range of technical standards. Many of the technical standards are already being agreed across the public sector as part of e-government, and we will adopt these standards for the NHS.

5.4 It is important that standards, once agreed, are used across the NHS, and we will introduce measures to ensure this. The NHS Information Standards Boards will have a key role. For example the Technical Standards Board has formally adopted the *Government Interoperability Framework standards*, together with the BS7799 Code of Practice for information security for application in the NHS. We will now be producing a migration plan to cover areas such as the introduction of the SMTP standard for e-mail and use of the XML standard for messaging. Agreeing to implement these standards will be a requirement of the corporate agreements between health communities and Regional Offices, and hence a condition of funding for IM&T investment.

Getting Connected

5.5   We are already well advanced in connecting GPs to the NHSnet – to date some 80% of GP practices have been connected. Over time connectivity will be extended to include other healthcare organisations such as NHS walk-in centres and GP out-of-hours co-operatives. We will ensure that all staff within the NHS have access to application and information services by March 2003. We have also been taking steps to improve the performance and reliability of the network. For example, considerable improvements have been made over recent months to the network infrastructure and to the messaging service, and further enhancements are planned, including:

- improving actual performance and resilience by raising service levels for message delivery and service availability, improved service reporting, anti "spamming" protection for all users, restriction of periods available for planned downtime, removal of delayed delivery messages

- enhancing support services by providing a comprehensive integrated second-line support service for GP practices, covering the Message Handling Service, local email systems and NHSnet, and improved support service reporting

- providing better address book services, including an interim web-based national directory service accessible to everyone who has access to NHSnet.

5.6   However, the requirements for access and sharing of information are far broader than just within the NHS. Local Authority Social Services, the voluntary sector and patients are among the partners with whom the NHS is working. Technological advances also have opened a range of possibilities for communication and networking to support new ways of providing health services.

5.7   The existing networking service contracts expire around 2003. As part of the re-procurement we are exploring the extent to which we will want to standardise the provision of core data and voice networking services. This includes provision for increased network bandwidth to support new requirements such as imaging, and other elements of infrastructure such as common products and managed services.

Ensuring Security and Confidentiality

5.8 Patients and the public must be assured that their information is held securely and shared according to appropriate legal, ethical and technical processes. Current initiatives will, however, lead to more sharing of information and this therefore increases the responsibility of professionals to protect the data they hold and access, and to preserve the confidentiality of this information.

5.9 Each organisation should now have a Caldicott guardian to oversee information flows, and it is important that this role is given due prominence. We have now agreed that the Caldicott principles will be extended to social care and are looking to achieve this by September 2001.

5.10 The main provisions of the Data Protection Act 1998 came into force in March 2000. The Act now covers all manual and electronic records. We are currently working on a major study into patient consent, and will publish the results of this study in April 2001.

5.11 Security of information is critical. We have adopted the BS7799 national standard for security in the NHS. This Code of Practice presents a range of information security management policies and practices, and is already widely used by UK businesses and other public sector bodies. NHS organisations will need to complete a gap analysis comparing existing practice against the national standard and produce their responses by June 2001, with a compliance audit of security arrangements to be completed by December 2001. We will also give consideration to how best to apply common national standards for security within social care providers.

5.12 Together with this information strategy update we are publishing an initial national cryptography support services strategy (available at *www.doh.gov.uk/ipu/strategy/crypto/index.htm*). This will lead to the procurement and implementation of a full Public-Key Infrastructure that will be available for use across the NHS by April 2002. Interim guidance on securing information flows is also now available.

Education and Training

5.13 Implementing the NHS Plan and *"Working Together with Health Information"* will bring about many changes in the education and training requirements of staff. Professional training will have more emphasis on supporting the redesigned care system and also on working with information and applying IT.

5.14 The fundamental role of information and IT signals a need for new skills – to agree best practice standards, collect and analyse data, and procure, develop and apply high quality information systems to support patient-centred care. Increasingly information-rich and IT literate patients will seek a change in their relationships with care staff. Clinical education is beginning to be underpinned by web-based learning technologies and can be enabled by new Human Resource systems. To maximise the benefits available to the NHS directly, and for new staff in the future, we must share the technologies and enable better access to systems between education centres and NHS organisations. Further integration between sectors and the development of e-learning will support lifelong learning to keep practitioner skills up to date.

5.15   Work is underway to build health information management and information technology into curricula for all healthcare professionals, including the new curriculum for nurses. It is vital that a valued part of the basic skills for clinical staff is the ability to use IT to manage information effectively. Significant progress has been made; most courses include health informatics modules, IT training and use of the Internet for knowledge management. A multi-professional standard for clinical education called *"Learning to Manage Health Information"* has been agreed with all of the mainstream professional and regulatory bodies. Together with Department of Health colleagues, the NHS Information Authority programme "Ways of Working with Information" team will help to facilitate the further implementation of this standard. The standard applies equally to trainees and existing staff. The Academy of Medical Royal Colleges has recently held a conference to determine how best to implement *Learning to Manage Health Information* and the *European Computer Driving Licence (ECDL).*

5.16   ECDL is the international standard which will be used to help improve basic computer skills of all NHS staff. ECDL has been favourably evaluated and plans for its roll out are being developed. ECDL is complementary to section 5 of *Learning to Manage Health Information* and will also feature in Individual Learning Accounts for non-professional health occupations. The Department of Health (HR Directorate) has initiated a pilot programme together with the University for industry (Ufi) to provide access to *Learn direct* training materials, including ECDL support materials, for non-professional staff in 13 NHS organisations. A key issue with ECDL is to manage its implementation in parallel with the development of local systems, and making use of relevant modules for different staff groups. Health informatics staff need to develop their professional skills too. The existing target is that 50% should either have, be studying for, or registered for, appropriate qualifications by March 2001.

5.17   The NHS Information Authority "Ways of Working with Information" programme will help NHS staff use and implement information management systems by:

- introducing programmes to develop the right skills in the right timescales for local communities and in the longer-term help to change the culture so that IM&T becomes a natural tool for healthcare professionals to use

- providing the right help through a network of regionally based Education and Development Advisers (EDAs) who will support local communities and LIS training co-ordinators in the development and implementation of their ETD plans

- setting up networks of information champions in each region who will be able to offer their expertise and experience to help develop LISs

- ensuring that every national programme is supported by appropriate, relevant and practical pre and post implementation products and services for use by local communities, starting with NSFs, procurement and information standards.

5.18   An important culture change initiative is commencing early in 2001 to help local health communities identify and deliver the information required for Clinical Governance. This will be facilitated through a partnership between the Information Policy Unit, Clinical Governance Support Team and the Ways of Working Programme. In addition an Academic Forum has been established to identify and work on key research issues and help to develop health informatics capabilities.

6 Supporting Implementation

- **Partnership**

- **Improving procurement and the market**

- **Exploiting the NHSknowledge base**

6.1   NHS Plan taskforces are in place to support implementation of the NHS Plan. Information management and IT underpins much of the work of these taskforces at a national level and work is in hand to deliver what they require.

6.2   For information and IT the emphasis remains on achieving local implementation of the national information strategy in support of the NHS Plan. The key roles will be:

- **National Information Policy Board** – together with chairs of information partnership fora and members from key DH policy divisions, the National Information Policy Board (NIPB) ensures that the IM&T aspects of NHS Plan taskforces are met. It oversees and advises on plans for the development and implementation of the strategy. An executive team of the NIPB, with membership from the Information Policy Unit, NHS Information Authority, Regional Heads of Information and DH Communications Directorate, will take corporate responsibility for supporting the implementation programme, corporate communications and the evaluation and sharing of good practice.

- **Information Policy Unit** – leading policy and strategic work on information supporting national policy development, in particular implementation of the NHS Plan. Co-ordination of policy development within the NHS Plan Taskforces and within other policy branches of the Department of Health. Responsible for the overall co-ordination and commissioning of the work programme of the NHS Information Authority and for ensuring that Regional Offices and local health communities have performance agreements in place with robust performance management arrangements.

- **Regional Offices** – ensuring national proposals are locally workable, highlight areas where further support would be beneficial in implementation, and communicate proposals to the field. Provide implementation support to NHS organisations locally, and manage performance in delivering the national strategy. Agree three-year performance agreements with local health communities for their Local Implementation Strategies. A range of performance measures will be developed to ensure the implementation of these agreements. One key requirement of such agreements will be the adoption of national standards.

- **NHS Information Authority** – delivering and managing the national products and services that supports *Information for Health* and specifically those components which can only or best be done at a national level. The products and services delivered will support patient care, operational services, strategic initiatives and development and innovation.

6.3   The NHS Plan sets out a completely new way of delivering healthcare. At a local level success is totally dependent on change management. There must be an active managerial role in resolving the problems and providing the resource to successfully apply information and IT in healthcare. In this climate the NHS must take every opportunity to share best practice and demonstrate real innovation.

6.4   To deliver a health service designed around the patient, local health and social care organisations need to work in partnership. The work on Local Implementation Strategies has established co-operative working amongst local teams who are now working on implementing the information strategy supported by corporate agreements and nationally agreed criteria, including targets and costed investment plans. Regional Offices are reviewing progress against the LIS traffic light system but in the longer term the information and IT national targets will form a key part of the overall national priorities. This means that local performance across the whole health community in implementing the information standards and infrastructure will be assessed and counted towards the 'green', 'yellow' or 'red' classification set out in the NHS Plan.

6.5   In addition to partnerships within the NHS and local health communities, we will develop new ways of working with other public services to ensure joined up service delivery to the citizen, with the private sector to develop an improved range of service delivery channels and with private healthcare providers to treat more NHS patients.

6.6   Delivering the objectives in the NHS Plan and *Information for Health* requires much improved relationships with the private sector. For too long the NHS has not been seen by suppliers as good to do business with. By making our objectives and targets clear, and backing this with substantial and sustained resources, we are sending a clear message that we want to work with the leading ICT suppliers. Both the provision and support of the national infrastructure services, and the development of a range of managed services through consortia working with local health communities, require a strong strategic relationship between the NHS and its private partners to be developed. At present the Computer Software and Services Association represents suppliers' interests on the National Information Policy Board. However, it is clear that we need to strengthen the means for involving a wider range of ICT product and service providers.

6.7   We need to create an environment of innovation by encouraging new ideas, sharing good practice and managing the risks. The purpose of innovating through information and IT is to transform the business processes. For the NHS this translates to new clinical practices and information flows and processes. The step change required by the NHS Plan, the expectations of patients and the public, and the pace of technological change demand a new approach to innovation. Standardisation and mandation will be required for key services and in key areas but innovation must be encouraged too. The best ideas can then be shared, adopted and taken forward for the whole NHS.

6.8   Nationally we have already commissioned projects looking at applications for digital TV, and for the electronic transfer of prescriptions, and we are looking at potential uses of smart cards. We are aware of new services around the provision of personal health records and e-pharmacy services, and many other local initiatives. NHS knowledge and library services are actively investigating partnerships with The British Library, the Higher Education community and The People's Network of public libraries to improve access to knowledge for NHS staff and the public alike. The aim of such projects is to test new technologies, concepts and ways of working.

6.9   Adopting innovation means adopting new ways of working. We will provide the opportunity for NHS and other public and private sector organisations to develop new ideas rapidly, in an assured NHS information systems environment that offers the opportunity of rapid deployment of successful innovation and hence rapid realisation of benefits. In these partnerships between private and public sector we will be adopting the incubator approach described by the Cabinet Office in their report *"Electronic Government Services for the 21st Century."*

Improving procurement and the market

6.10   We are taking forward the conclusions of the *NHS IM&T procurement review* published in May 2000. In new and developing areas – such as appointment booking services, the electronic transfer of prescriptions or e-pharmacy services – our approach will be to develop understanding of requirements and the practical implementation issues through incubator programmes and by piloting through local projects. The learning from these will shape the requirements for later development and subsequent national implementation. For example we are developing a Strategic Outline Case for electronic booking systems building on the learning from pilots. This will help determine the preferred national solution.

6.11   Within more mature areas – such as hospital electronic patient record systems, where significant change management is required at a local level – the strategy will be to move forwards through local initiatives. We will focus on the common requirements and solutions that are evident from region-wide and national assessments, and will also seek to reduce the number and length of different procurement exercises. By undertaking joint procurements, we will create framework arrangements that can be used by sets of Trusts or, preferably, health communities, who may be at earlier stages in the implementation cycle. The work of the South West regional acute EPR procurement is an example of such an approach. It is clear that, with proper arrangements for project support, the benefits of consortia working are becoming accepted. Typically, a prime contractor will be responsible for overall delivery, working with a range of system and service suppliers. Based on such practical experience, we will support the development of specifications and evaluations to enable lists of such systems and service suppliers to be maintained nationally. In these more mature areas, projects must conform to agreed national and international standards to ensure that the selected products and services can interwork and be quickly implemented throughout the NHS.

6.12   In more established areas where there is a range of sophisticated products and services, we will use standard catalogues for products – such as hardware, core office systems software etc – and implement common national solutions in areas such as financial services, payroll and human resource management. The NHS Purchasing and Supply Agency are working with the Office of Government Commerce to develop the NHS-Cat catalogue. This will be a key resource to help the quick and efficient procurement of commodity items, while the national payroll/HR project is working to procure and implement a national payroll service for the NHS.

6.13   In all areas we are ensuring that we learn from the procurement experiences across government in line with the recommendations of the report *"Successful IT – Modernising Government in Action"*, a review of major government IT projects. This involves the development of Strategic Outline Cases for major investments as well as adopting a process of independent gateway reviews for key projects.

Exploiting the NHS knowledge base

6.14   The NHS is a brand name that is recognised internationally. The quantity, quality, and hence value of the information and knowledge assets associated with that brand, should be carefully used for the benefit of the patients of the NHS and also across wider global healthcare markets. Patients and staff will benefit from an open and inclusive knowledge base and learning network. There will need to be a transparency in developing the content for NHS branded information and systems to clearly demonstrate our objectivity. While there are major opportunities in exploiting NHS knowledge resources, we will need to ensure that the values of the brand are not put at risk through inappropriate partnerships.

7 Delivering the Information Core

- **Connecting NHS staff**
- **Delivering information – Information Services**
- **Delivering information – Electronic Records and Booking**
- **Delivering information – National Applications**
- **Local planning and preparation**

7.1   Much clearer communication with the service and the public is needed on expectations, targets and outcomes. This also calls for more focused control over an information and IT work programme that is managed according to agreed priorities. This final section contains details of the key targets to be achieved over the next four years, in order to meet the commitments contained in the NHS Plan in relation to information systems. These should be seen as "latest dates" and local plans should aim to meet these targets as soon as possible.

7.2   The targets do not undermine the value of the existing or proposed *Local Implementation Strategies* (LISs) work that health communities are already undertaking. The overall direction of travel provided by *Information for Health* is reinforced by the NHS Plan. The new emphasis is on realigning priorities and increasing the pace of delivery to ensure we have, for example, electronic booking of appointments, NHS staff connected to NHSnet and patients able to access their own medical records more quickly than envisaged in 1998.

7.3   *The process of updating LISs* and their associated implementation plans will need to reflect these targets and ensure that where there is scope for local options, the LIS supports the local health and healthcare service priorities as set out in the local Health Improvement Programme. LISs and related local investment plans will need to be re-calibrated to address the amended timetable and take into account the additional resources being made available. LIS communities are required to provide these updates by 31 March 2001. They will be subject to a process of local and national evaluation as with the full LIS.

7.4   From the evaluation of full LIS's in summer 2000, there are two common areas for improvement, namely the need for much greater involvement of clinical staff in the planning and implementation process, and more innovative thinking around the development of cross-cutting health informatics services. Improvements in both these areas are expected, and will be closely monitored as part of the 2001 LIS evaluation process.

7.5   The performance agreement between Regional Offices and local health communities will ensure that local plans are realistic and sufficiently detailed to allow progress to be monitored against all targets during the implementation period.

Stage 1: Connecting NHS staff

7.6   The aim of these accelerated targets is to provide initial desktop access for all relevant NHS Trust staff to NHSnet and the Internet. The working definition for desktop access is based around the provision of a core set of NHS tools:

- E-mail

- web browser

- directory services including NHS National Address Book and user authentication services.

	National Percentages by Date				
	31/03/01	31/03/02	31/03/03	31/03/04	31/03/05
	Target for all NHS Staff				
Desk top access to basic e-mail, browsing and directory services for all clinical and support staff in NHS Trusts	25	100			
Provide remaining NHS staff with access to the above			100		
Submit Address Books and produce interim centrally managed NHS Address Book	100				
Access to X500 conformant NHS Address Book directory for all connected staff		100			

7.7   To enable implementation the following central actions will be completed:

> November 2000 Formal adoption of e-GIF conformant standards including those for E-mail, browser software.
>
> March 2001 Publish migration plan for existing systems – e.g. E-mail messaging – to move to new standards.
>
> June 2001 Publish policy on use of proprietary office systems software and their conformance to e-GIF standards and NHS requirements. Simultaneously guidance on procurement arrangements will be published.
>
> March 2003 Complete migration to new standards for all NHS users.

7.8   These basic tools will enable NHS staff to use:

- NHS-wide and local web servers to access guidance, procedures, protocols and other services e.g. through NeLH and e-recruitment, e-learning and updating their own personal records

- E-mail systems to communicate with other NHS staff and non-NHS organisations e.g. Local Authority Social Services.

7.9   Access must be provided conveniently within the normal place of work. It is not possible to dictate centrally what this means; it will be different for different groups of staff. Only local organisations can decide on the exact requirements for their staff and many are well down the road of doing so. A medical secretary will almost certainly require a dedicated desktop PC including other facilities, especially word processing. A junior doctor is likely to need access in a number of locations such as wards, clinics and offices, depending on his/her "range". A community nurse may need a hand-held device with mobile links. In all cases the geographical distribution of service provision will be a key factor and local plans will be reflected in LISs.

7.10   Local communities and individual organisations may prioritise the implementation by different staff groups, but LIS plans for the 2001 review must address the overall target of having network access for all NHS staff by 31 March 2003. These implementation arrangements must include plans to ensure all staff have adequate training.

7.11   The following specific targets remain for general practice:

	National Percentages by Date				
	31/03/01	31/03/02	31/03/03	31/03/04	31/03/05
GP Practices to be computerised	98	100			
GP Practices with NHSnet connection	95	100			
GP Practices with LANs connected to NHSnet e.g. desktop access	90	100			

7.12   Decisions on the targets for the connection of other primary care practitioners and social care professionals will be made based on the Strategic Outline Case for the re-procurement of NHS networking services to be completed by March 2001. For example, to meet the aim of having routine electronic prescribing in the community by 2004 will require access to networking services for pharmacists.

7.13   In addition, comprehensive arrangements for sharing information between NHS and Local Authority Social Services will need to be completely operational by March 2005. The following products to be delivered by 31 January 2001 will facilitate cross sector working:

• a toolkit to develop local protocols for sharing information (*live on DH website from 6 November 2000*)

• NHSnet Code of Connection to include Social Services

• *national cryptography support services strategy.*

Stage 2A: Delivering Information – Information Services

7.14   The developments on NHS Direct Online, nhs.uk and the National electronic Library for Health have already been outlined in the box on page 24.

	National Percentages by Date				
	31/03/01	31/03/02	31/03/03	31/03/04	31/03/05
Online public information on availability of NHS services (1)	100				

Notes:

1. The initial service to support the provision of information to the public is based on a core set of information (*www.doh.gov.uk/ipu/whatnew/eguide.html*) that will be extended over time to meet other NHS Plan commitments.

Stage 2B: Delivering Information – Electronic Records and Booking

7.15   The original *Information for Health* targets for full Electronic Patient Records and 24 hour emergency Electronic Health Records remain unchanged. There are new requirements for providing booked appointments for patients. The priorities for basic connectivity detailed above are an essential platform to achieve these targets.

	National Percentages by Date				
	31/03/01	31/03/02	31/03/03	31/03/04	31/03/05
Acute EPR Level 3(1)	10	35		75	100
Integrated Primary and Community EPR (2)			25	50	100
Emergency Care EHR (3)					100
All bookings from GPs to outpatients or from outpatients to daycase or inpatients to be made electronically (4)					100
Electronic transfer of all biochemistry, haematology and microbiology test results (5)		60(7)			
Electronic transfer of all radiology reports and discharge summaries between hospital and GP's (5)			100		
All NHS Pathology laboratories to be connected to NHSnet (6)	100				
All Pathology results sent to GPs to contain NHS Number		100			

Notes:

1. Acute EPR level 3 – this target will be described in a clearer way along the lines of: "X number of acute trusts in each region must have introduced an EPR system capable of the following functionality – A, B, C – by the given deadline". The NHSIA have

published consultation documents on the definition of EPR level 3 in November 2000; they are available at: *www.nhsia.nhs.uk/erdip/*

2. Integrated primary and community EPR – policy decisions on architecture and content will be published by the Information Policy Unit in September 2001 following an assessment of the interim outcomes of the ERDIP demonstrators.

3. Emergency care EHR – there will be a national solution for the emergency care EHR. A policy statement on this will be published by the Information Policy Unit in September 2001 following an assessment of the interim outcomes of the relevant ERDIP demonstrators.

4. A national Strategic Outline Case – to be published by the National Patient Access Team in March 2001 – will identify how this is to be achieved and detailed implementation guidance for the NHS will follow.

5. An impact assessment of HL7 version 3 and its applicability to clinical communications across the NHS will be undertaken by the NHSIA, with a report published in March 2001.

6. Connection to NHSnet for basic access – e-mail and web browsing.

7. 60% by 31 March 2002, 100% by 31 December 2002

Stage 2C: Delivering Information – National Applications

7.16   Providing access to the first generation of national applications for all connected staff will include:

	National Percentages by Date				
	31/03/01	31/03/02	31/03/03	31/03/04	31/03/05
All electronic communications about patients to include their NHS Number verified by NSTS (1)			100		
Online access to national codes for GPs and consultants	100				
National NHS payroll and integrated HR system (2)				100	
All outpatient datasets to be transmitted through NWCS (3)		100			

Notes:

1. This applies to all authorised NHS staff dealing face-to-face with patients or their records, care plans diagnostic tests and reporting of tests.

2. The implementation of an integrated HR and payroll system will be highly dependent on the effective completion of basic connectivity and robust authentication procedures described earlier.

3. The aim is that all providers should submit outpatient records via the NWCS from 1 October 2001. Additional datasets to be transferred through NWCS will be considered, with waiting lists as a priority.

Stage 3: Local planning and preparation

7.17   In addition to the 'hard deliverables' concerned with completing "network NHS" there are processes and preparatory work to be completed:

	National Percentages by Date				
	31/03/01	31/03/02	31/03/03	31/03/04	31/03/05
LIS update (1)	100				
Integration of information strategies to support NSF topics into LIS development within 6 months of the publication of the relevant strategy (2)		100			
Application of Working in Partnership toolkit (3)		100			
Production of local education, training and development strategies	100				

Notes:

1. Detailed guidance on scope of update is being issued by the Information Policy Unit in conjunction with this document.
2. The LIS update must include plans to support the implementation of the Cancer Information Strategy and the NHS Cancer Plan. The target dates for publication of the remaining information strategies are mental health – January 2001; coronary heart disease and older people – March 2001; and Diabetes – with the National Service Framework.
3. Each LIS community will demonstrate how it is developing collaborative working through use of the toolkit, online version available at *www.doh.gov.uk/ipu/pspp/partner.htm*

APPENDIX 4
USE AND DISCLOSURE OF HEALTH DATA

Guidance on the Application of the Data Protection Act 1998

May 2002

Table of Contents

Information Commissioner's Foreword

The Data Protection Act 1998 presents a number of significant challenges to data controllers in the health sector. Over the course of the last year, I have seen a significant increase in the number of requests for assistance from individuals. At the same time I have been asked to consider issues arising out the Department of Health electronic patient records project, issues in relation to cancer and other disease registries, and issues in relation to the use of patient data in research. Frequently these requests for advice have significant implications for the NHS as a whole and the Department of Health as well as for patients.

It seems to me that there are several reasons for the increase in requests for assistance and advice. Firstly there has been an extension of the scope of Data Protection from purely automated records to many classes of manual records. Whereas the 1984 Act only applied to computerised records, the 1998 Act applies fully to all patient records whether they are held on computer or in paper files, and whether they consist of hand written case notes or x-rays.

Secondly, it is clear that many practitioners are confused between the requirements of the Data Protection Act and those of the various regulatory and representative bodies within the sector including the GMC, MRC, and BMA. To some extent the advice issued by these different bodies may reflect their different roles. To some extent it may also reflect misunderstandings of the requirements of the Act. It is a common misconception, for instance, that the Act always requires the consent of data subjects to the processing of their data. At the same time, as private litigation increases throughout society, many health service bodies have adopted a more cautious approach towards the use and disclosure of patient data, fearing that uses and disclosures of data which previously seemed unexceptionable might attract action for a breach of confidence.

Thirdly, the demands that are placed on the health service are greater and more varied than ever before. Health Authorities, NHS Trusts and individual practitioners are increasingly involved in inter-agency initiatives, whether in the context of the Crime and Disorder Act or the joint delivery of health and social care with local authority social service departments. Meanwhile, the creation of a national system of electronic health records is likely to raise fresh questions about who is responsible for those records and who should be allowed access to them.

If steps are not taken to clarify the ground rules, then the uncertainty experienced by clinicians and NHS organisations may translate into concerns on the part of patients as to who has access to their records and on what basis their personal data are processed. In that context I welcome wholeheartedly statements by Department of Health Ministers that in the foreseeable future all processing of patient records should be on the basis of informed consent. I also welcome the decision of the NHS Executive to begin work on development of a Code of Practice that is aimed at producing coherent practical guidance for clinicians and health service bodies incorporating the different standards emanating from the different professional and representative bodies. The guidance that I have published is more limited in its ambition. My aim has been to clarify the minimum requirements of the Data Protection Act, providing answers to frequently asked questions such as:

- Is patient consent necessary for processing?
- If so, in what circumstances?
- If so, in what form?
- When is it necessary to anonymise data?
- When is it necessary to pseudonymise data?

Although as far as possible the Guidance attempts to provide practical examples of the steps that should be taken in order to achieve compliance with the requirements of the Act, the audience for the Guidance is not primarily practitioners but data protection officers, Caldicott Guardians and those charged with the development of the IT infrastructure of the NHS. It is, in other words a somewhat technical document that seeks to explain the enforceable requirements of the Data Protection Act rather than to describe "good practice".

The term "enforceable requirements" refers to the powers given to me by the Act to take action against data controllers whom I consider to be in breach of any of the eight Data Protection Principles in Schedule 1 of the Act. The Act does not, however, require that I take enforcement action on each occasion that I consider that there has been a breach. Before serving an enforcement notice I will not only measure the performance of the data controller against the standard set out in the guidance but also consider, as the Act requires, whether the actions of the data controller have caused damage or distress to any individual. I shall also have regard to the circumstances of different data controllers. For instance, as is explained in the section of the Guidance dealing with privacy enhancing technologies, in many cases it may be possible to process patient data, for instance for research or administrative purposes, without having access to the data which would identify particular patients. While I would not necessarily expect each GP practice to develop its own IT system capable of concealing the identities of patients from those who do not need to know them, I do expect those developing IT systems for use by GPs to build in such a capability and I would certainly consider action against a GP (or any other data controller) who did not make use of the features available on a system for maximising the privacy of patients.

Finally, I would like to thank all those who have contributed towards the development of this guidance. Some seventy responses were received to the initial consultation paper issued in May 2001. Since a number of these were received from representative bodies, the number of organisations who had input was actually much greater. I would also particularly like to thank those individuals and organisations who attended the consultative seminar which I held in October of last year. While there will inevitably be issues upon which I am asked to provide further clarification, I am certain that without the help of all those who contributed to the consultation I would have faced a far greater number of such requests.

Elizabeth France
May 2002

Chapter 1: Introduction

Scope of the Guidance

The Data Protection Act 1998 gives effect in UK law to EC Directive 95/46/EC, and introduces Eight Data Protection Principles that set out standards of information handling. These standards apply to all data controllers who process personal data. This guidance is concerned with the application of the Act with regards to the processing of information contained within 'health records'. The term, "Processing", includes the collection, use, and disclosure of personal data. The guidance is limited, in the main, to the requirements of the First Data Protection Principle and the Second Data Protection Principle. Further general advice regarding the other Principles, which cover such matters as data quality, rights of access, and security, can be found in *"The Data Protection Act 1998 – Legal Guidance"*, which is available on the Information Commissioner's website at ***www.informationcommissioner.gov.uk***.

The term 'health record' is defined by Section 68 of the Act, and means any record which:

- consists of information relating to the physical or mental health or condition of an individual, and

- has been made by or on behalf of a health professional in connection with the care of that individual.

The term 'health professional' is also defined by the Act, and the definition is included in Appendix 2.

This Guidance will be of most value to individuals within organisations (including both the public and private sector) whose responsibilities include data protection, privacy and confidentiality issues. These may include data protection officers, Caldicott Guardians, or legal advisers. The Guidance sets out the requirements of the law and in some cases provides an indication of the issues that data controllers will need to consider when fulfilling their obligations under the Act. The Guidance also aims to provide an indication of the standard which the Information Commissioner will seek to enforce. It is not the intention of this Guidance to provide specific advice on all the possible uses and disclosures of patient information. Data controllers will need to apply the general advice provided here to their specific situations. Box 1 gives an indication of the areas upon which guidance is provided. These are treated more fully in Appendix 1.

Box 1

Examples of uses and disclosures of personal data

a) Care & Treatment

- Routine record keeping, consultation of records etc, in the course of the provision of care and treatment;

- Processing of records in the event of a medical emergency;

- Disclosures made by one health professional or organisation to another, e.g. where a GP refers a patient to a specialist;

- Clinical audit e.g. the monitoring of a patient care pathway against existing standards and benchmarks.

b) Administration

- Processing for administrative purposes, e.g. disclosure by a GP made in order to receive payment for treatment provided;

- Administrative audit, which may include studies designed to improve the efficiency of the NHS as an organisation, e.g. to support decisions about the allocation of resources.

c) Research & Teaching

- Statutory disclosures to disease registries and for epidemiological research;

- Non-statutory disclosures to disease registries and for epidemiological research;

- Clinical trials;

- Hospital-based teaching;

- University-based teaching.

d) Use and disclosures for non-health purposes

- Disclosures for Crime and Disorder Act 1998 purposes;

- Disclosures to the police;

- Disclosures to hospital chaplains;

- Disclosures to the media.

This list is not exhaustive. It is likely that data controllers will need to apply the requirements of the Act to uses and disclosures of health data that are not listed above.

Chapter 2: First Data Protection Principle

The First Data Protection Principle states:

> "Personal data shall be processed fairly and lawfully and, in particular, shall not be processed unless –
>
> a)   at least one of the conditions in Schedule 2 is met, and
>
> b)   in the case of sensitive personal data, at least one of the conditions in Schedule 3 is also met"

The conditions in Schedules 2 and 3, referred to above, are listed in Appendix 2.

It is possible to identify a number of separate, albeit cumulative, requirements of this Principle:

- The requirement to satisfy a condition in Schedule 2 and Schedule 3;
- The requirement to collect personal data fairly;
- The requirement to process personal data lawfully.

The requirement to satisfy a condition in Schedule 2 and Schedule 3

In all cases data controllers must satisfy at least one of the conditions in Schedule 2 of the Act. In the context of health sector data controllers, the most relevant Schedule 2 conditions are likely to be:

- Processing with the consent of the data subject;

- Processing necessary to protect the vital interests of the data subject;

- Processing which is necessary for the exercise of functions of a public nature exercised in the public interest by any person;

- Processing which is necessary for the purposes of the legitimate interests pursued by the data controller or those of a third party to whom the data are disclosed, except where the processing is prejudicial to the rights and freedoms or legitimate interests of the data subject.

In practice, it is unlikely to be difficult to satisfy one of these conditions. The focus of this section of the Guidance is therefore on the Schedule 3 processing conditions, at least one of which must be satisfied when processing sensitive personal data. "Sensitive data" is defined in the Act and includes data that relates to the physical or mental health of data subjects. No distinction is drawn in the Act between, say, data relating to the mental health of patients and data relating to minor physical injuries: they are all sensitive.

The most relevant Schedule 3 conditions are likely to be:

- Processing with the explicit consent of the data subject;

- Processing necessary to protect the vital interests of the data subject or another person, where it is not possible to get consent;

- Processing necessary for the purpose of, or in connection with, legal proceedings (including prospective legal proceedings), obtaining legal advice, or is otherwise necessary for the purposes of establishing, exercising or defending legal rights;

- The processing is necessary for medical purposes and is undertaken by a health professional or a person owing a duty of confidentiality equivalent to that owed by a health professional.

The Act provides that included within the term 'medical purposes' are preventative medicine, medical diagnosis, medical research, the provision of care and treatment, and the management of healthcare services. This definition, with the exception of medical research, is taken from the Directive from which the Act is derived. The Commissioner considers that the term 'vital interests' refers to matters of life and death.

The Schedule 3 conditions have been supplemented by further conditions set out in the Data Protection (Processing of Sensitive Personal Data) Order 2000. The most likely conditions for the purposes of this Guidance are:

- Processing of medical data or data relating to ethnic origin for monitoring purposes;

- Processing in the substantial public interest, necessary for the purpose of research whose object is not to support decisions with respect to any particular data subject otherwise than with the explicit consent of the data subject and which is unlikely to cause substantial damage or substantial distress to the data subject or any other person.

The Necessity Test

Many of the conditions for processing set out in Schedule 2 and Schedule 3 specify that processing must be *necessary* for the purpose stated. In order to satisfy one of the conditions other than processing with consent, data controllers must be able to show that it would not be possible to achieve their purposes with a reasonable degree of ease without the processing of *personal* data. Where data controllers are able to achieve, with a reasonable degree of ease, a purpose using data from which the personal identifiers have been removed, this is the course of action that they must pursue. This may require the use of Privacy Enhancing Technologies (PETs) – Box below. What constitutes a 'reasonable degree of ease' is to be determined by taking into consideration issues including the technology available, and the form in which the personal data are held.

The Commissioner takes the view that when considering the issue of necessity, data controllers must consider objectively whether:

- Such purposes can be achieved only by the processing of personal data; and

- The processing is proportionate to the aim pursued.

This aspect of the First Principle is reinforced by the Third Data Protection Principle, which states that:

> "Personal data shall be adequate, relevant and not excessive in relation to the purpose or purposes for which they are processed".

The disclosure of personal data where this is not actually necessary would be likely to contravene this Principle.

Box 2

Privacy Enhancing Technologies (PETs)

In a general sense, the term "PET" is used to refer to an IT design philosophy which seeks to deploy new technology in ways which enhance rather than undermine privacy. From this standpoint, the use of techniques such as encryption, password control and other measures designed to ensure that data are guarded with appropriate security can all be regarded as privacy enhancing technologies. Privacy, however, is not limited to security and confidentiality. A Privacy Enhancing approach to database design might allow the holding of patient preferences (e.g. consent to be contacted in connection with medical research), might prompt a clinician to check the personal details of a patient who has not visited a surgery for some years, and might force the periodic review of older records.

More specifically PETs have become associated with systems designed to protect the identity of patients by substituting true identifiers such as name, address or National Health Number with pseudonyms. The starting point is the implied requirement of Schedule 2 and 3 of the Act that, in the absence of consent, personal data should only be processed where it is necessary to do so. If it is never necessary to know the identity of the individuals to whom personal data relates, then the data should be anonymised by removing all personal identifiers. Anonymisation is a permanent process and once anonymised, it will never be possible to link the data to particular individuals.

However, permanent anonymisation may not always be acceptable. For instance a researcher may have no need to know the identity of the patients suffering from a particular condition. He or she may, however, need to know that the patient who was diagnosed with the condition on a particular date is the same patient who was diagnosed with a different condition on another date. Pseudonymisation, sometimes described as "reversible anonymisation" provides a solution. In effect a computer system is used to substitute true patient identifiers with pseudonyms. The true identities are not, however, discarded but retained in a secure part of the computer system allowing the original data to be reconstituted as and when this is required. Typically those making day-to-day uses of pseudonymised data would not have the "keys" allowing the data to be reconstituted.

Potentially there are many different applications for such PETs. For instance they might allow researchers to make more extensive use of medical records without increasing the risk of the misuse or accidental disclosure of patient details. They might prevent support staff from gaining access to information about the medical condition of patients while allowing access to the information necessary to perform administrative tasks.

The Commissioner expects that consideration will be given to the deployment of PETs in all significant new IT developments within the Health Service. She would also expect that data controllers within the Health Service make use of any privacy enhancing features of the software and hardware which they use.

The requirement to collect personal data fairly

The Data Protection Principles are listed in Part 1 of Schedule 1 of the Act. Part 2 of Schedule 1 contains further statutory interpretation of the Act. Paragraph 2 of Part 2 sets out the obligation on data controllers to provide certain information to data subjects when collecting their personal data:

- The identity of the data controller;

- The identity of any representative nominated by the data controller for the purposes of the Act;

- The purpose or purposes for which the data are to be processed; and

- Any further information which is necessary, having regard to the specific circumstances in which the data are or are to be processed, to enable the processing in respect of the data subject to be fair.

These details are often referred to as "fair processing information", "the fair processing code", or the "fair collection code". In this Guidance we refer to these details as "fair processing information".

The question of the nominated representative of the data controller is highly unlikely to arise in the context of health records, and is not therefore considered here. The other three requirements are considered separately, before discussing the timing and the level of detail to be provided.

Identity of the data controller

Care should be taken to ensure that the data subject knows the identity of the data controller(s) that will process his or her data. Information as to the identity of the data controller should be reasonably specific (e.g. a GPs practice, a NHS Trust etc). "The NHS" or "The Health Service" are not legal entities and therefore cannot be data controllers. Within a GP practice the assumption of data subjects is probably that the practice as a whole is the data controller and that other members of the practice may have access to their records. If there is any doubt, e.g. if a number of GP practices share the same premises, it is the duty of the GP practice to ensure that the patient knows the true position.

Data controllers must also be aware that with increased multi-agency working and initiatives (e.g. between a Trust and a social services department), it may not be immediately clear to data subjects as to who the data controller actually is. Indeed, there may be more than one data controller, in which case the identity of all data controllers should be communicated to data subjects.

Purpose or purposes of processing

When explaining the purpose or purposes for which information is to be processed, data controllers must strike a balance between providing an unnecessary amount of detail and providing information in too general terms. An explanation to the effect that personal data are to be processed for 'health care purposes' would be too general. On the other hand, an explanation that explained all the administrative systems in which patient data might be recorded, the use of data for diagnosis, for treatment etc would be excessive. (An explanation which is not sufficiently detailed is unlikely, in any event, to be sufficient to obtain the consent of the data subject to the processing of data should this be required. The question of consent is considered in more detail in Chapter 4).

Other information necessary to make the processing fair

The Act provides no guidance as to what further information should be provided to data subjects in order to make the processing of their data fair. Clearly this will vary from case to case and from patient to patient depending upon levels of understanding of how the NHS operates, command of English and the sensitivity of the data in question. However, among the information that it may be necessary to provide is the following:

*   Information as to what data are to be or have been recorded, where this is in doubt. Patients are likely to expect that basic information will be recorded as to diagnosis and treatment. They may, however, be surprised to find that other information has been recorded whether this is an opinion of a doctor or the circumstances surrounding an injury. Unless patients have a reasonably clear idea of what is recorded about them, any consent to other uses or disclosures of their data may not be valid.

- Information as to specific disclosures. Given the sensitivity of medical data, data subjects should be informed of any non-routine disclosures of their data.

- Information as to whether any secondary uses or disclosures of data are optional. Where patients have a choice as to whether to provide information, to allow its disclosure to third parties or to object to certain uses or disclosures, then the requirement of fairness suggests that these choices should be brought to their attention.

How much fair processing information should be provided?

Concern has been expressed that the fair processing rules may require the provision of very large amounts of information in which patients have no real interest. In the Commissioner's view this concern is misplaced. In effect the fair processing information provided should achieve two basic purposes:

- It should provide sufficient information to allow the patients to exercise their rights in relation to their data. Hence patients should be told who will process their data, including any disclosures of personal data (which will allow them to make subject access requests), whether it must be supplied (which will allow them to opt-out if they wish), and what information is contained in their record (which will allow them to give meaningful consent to its processing.)

- It should provide sufficient information to allow the individual to assess the risks to him or her in providing their data, in consenting to their wider use, in choosing not to object to their processing etc. This should have at least two consequences for data controllers. It should become clear that fair processing notices do not need to contain a large amount of detail about routine, administrative uses of data. It should also become clear that researchers engaged in open-ended studies are not prevented by the Act from soliciting patient data on the grounds that their fair processing notices cannot be sufficiently detailed. Fair processing notices in this case should simply need to make clear that the research in question is indeed open-ended, leaving the individual to assess the risk.

It may also be helpful to bear in mind that the fair processing rules do not mean that patients must be provided with information that they are known to already possess.

When should fair processing information be provided?

It is likely that there will be a number of standard purposes for which the personal data of all patients entering a hospital or registering with a GP will be processed, information about which can be provided to patients at the outset of the episode of care. In particular, patients may need to be told about typical flows of data between different NHS bodies. This information is relatively timeless and it is appropriate that patients are given it at an early opportunity. It would certainly be good practice to remind patients of this information from time to time, for instance by ensuring that leaflets containing the relevant information are available to patients.

Some patients may subsequently have their personal data processed for a number of additional purposes e.g. information about a cancer diagnosis may be passed to a cancer registry, or information may be passed to social services. Those patients who will have their personal data processed for these additional purposes will need to be provided with this further information, in order to satisfy the fair processing requirements. This type of information is specific to particular patients at particular times and should be given in context, at a time when individuals are able to make sense of it.

How should the fair processing information be given?

The provision of 'fair processing information' by means of a poster in the surgery or waiting room or by a notice in the local paper etc is unlikely to be sufficient to meet the requirements of the Act since not all patients will see or be able to understand such information. Such methods may, however, be used to supplement other forms of communication. Methods by which the fair processing information may be provided include a standard information leaflet, information provided face to face in the course of a consultation, information included with an appointment letter from a hospital or clinic, or a letter sent to a patient's home. The effort involved in providing this information may be minimised by integrating the process with existing procedures. Many GP practices, for instance, already provide leaflets to patients about how the practice operates. Such leaflets could easily incorporate the fair processing information. Doctors may be able to easily provide specific information to patients in the course of consultations. Only where such an opportunity does not present itself will it be necessary to contact patients separately, for instance, if they are to be invited to participate in a programme of research involving the disclosure of their medical records to a researcher who may wish to interview patients with particular medical conditions.

Obtaining data from a person other than the data subject

In many cases medical information will be obtained directly from the patient either because it has been supplied by the patient (e.g. a description of symptoms) or has been obtained by a medical examination conducted by the person creating the record (e.g. an observation of symptoms). In a significant proportion of cases, however, data will be obtained by other means, whether from a third party or generated by the person creating the record (e.g. a medical opinion based on symptoms presented).

The Act recognises that the provision of fair processing information when data are obtained other than from the data subject presents some difficulties. The following exceptions from the provision of the fair processing information may only be relied upon by data controllers where they have obtained personal data from someone other than the data subject. It should be stressed that the ability to rely on an exemption does not absolve the data controller from the overriding duty to process personal data fairly.

The exceptions are:

*   Where providing the fair processing information would involve a disproportionate effort; or

*   Where it is necessary for the data controller to record the information to be contained in the data, or to disclose the data, to comply with any legal obligation to which the data controller is subject, other than an obligation imposed by contract.

The term 'disproportionate effort' is not defined by the Act. In assessing what does or does not amount to disproportionate effort, the starting point must be that data controllers are **not** generally exempt from providing the fair processing information because they have not obtained data directly from the data subject. What does or does not amount to disproportionate effort is a question of fact to be determined in each and every case.

In deciding this, the Commissioner will take into account a number of factors, including the nature of the data, the length of time and the cost involved to the data controller in providing the information. The fact that the data controller has had to expend a substantial amount of effort and/or cost in providing the information does not necessarily mean that the Commissioner will reach the decision that the data controller can legitimately rely upon the disproportionate effort exception. In certain circumstances, the Commissioner would consider that such an effort could reasonably be expected. The above factors will always be balanced against the effect on the data subject and in this respect a relevant consideration would be the extent to which the data subject already knows about the processing of his or her personal data by the data controller.

Data controllers should note that the Data Protection (Conditions Under Paragraph 3 of Part II of Schedule 1) Order 2000 provides that any data controller claiming the benefit of the disapplication of the requirement to provide fair processing information must still provide this information to any individual who requests it. In addition a data controller who does not provide fair processing information because to do so would involve disproportionate effort must keep a record of the reasons why he believes the disapplication of the fair processing requirements is necessary.

In practice, the Commissioner thinks that it is increasingly unlikely that NHS data controllers will be able to rely successfully upon these provisions. While there will be many cases in which, say, a consultant, receives personal data from a person other than the data subject, for instance his or her GP, the GP will have obtained the data directly from the patient and will have therefore provided the necessary fair processing information. There is no need, in other words, for the consultant to rely upon the exception since the patient will already be in possession of the fair processing information.

One area, however, where the exception is likely to be of assistance is that of records created before the enactment of data protection legislation. The Commissioner would generally accept that it would involve disproportionate effort to write to all existing patients to provide the fair processing information. However, that information should be available to patients when they attend surgeries and clinics and would have to be given in the event of any non-routine uses or disclosures of personal data.

The exception may also be relevant for those carrying out records based research where records were created in the past without the intention of using them for research purposes. (This issue is considered in greater detail in the following chapter under the heading "The Research Exemption".)

Cases where the requirement to provide fair processing information does not apply

There are a number of circumstances in which the requirement to provide the fair processing information does not apply.

- Section 29 of the Act permits uses or disclosures of personal data for the purpose of the prevention or detection of crime or the prosecution or apprehension of offenders, even though the data subject was not informed of those uses or disclosures, if to inform the data subject might prejudice that purpose. This may be of relevance in the context of combating fraud and corruption, e.g. in circumstances where it may be alleged that a GP has sought payment from a Health Authority for treatment which was not given, or where it is alleged that a patient has claimed free treatment to which he or she is not entitled. The exemption may also justify the disclosure of medical information to the police investigating an alleged assault on a member of staff.

- Section 31(2)(a)(iii) of the Act may allow for the disclosure of personal data without a prior explanation having been given to the data subject if the disclosure is necessary for protecting members of the public against "dishonesty, malpractice or other seriously improper conduct by, or the unfitness or incompetence of, persons authorised to carry on any profession or activity". This would appear to allow disclosures, in certain cases, of patient data to bodies responsible for maintaining professional standards.

- Section 31(4)(iii) allows the disclosure of personal data to the Health Service Commissioners (the Ombudsman) if not to do so would prejudice the discharge of the functions of those bodies.

- Section 35 allows the disclosure of information without breach of, among other things, the First, Second and Third Principles where the disclosure is a requirement of law or for the purpose of establishing, exercising or defending legal rights.

Although the exemptions may be relevant in some cases, they are unlikely to be the basis for the routine or wholesale processing of data without the provision of the information specified in the fair processing information to the data subject. In many cases, even though an exemption is apparently available, it would be wrong to rely upon it since it would be unnecessary to do so.

An example would be a disclosure of personal data for medical research purposes made in accordance with an order under s.60 of the Health and Social Care Act 2001 (applicable only in England and Wales). An order might specify, for instance, that all clinicians making a diagnosis of cancer must make a report to a cancer registry. While superficially s.35 suggests that fair processing information need not be given to the patient since the disclosure is a requirement of the law, in fact it would not be proper to rely upon the exemption since to provide the fair processing information would not be inconsistent with the disclosure.

By contrast, a hospital might decide to disclose to the police relevant parts of the medical record of a patient who had assaulted a member of staff even though no fair processing information had been given, since in that case there would be prejudice to the s.29 purpose of the disclosure if the normal rules were followed.

The requirement to process personal data lawfully

In addition to the requirement to satisfy a condition in Schedule 2 and Schedule 3 of the Act, there is a general requirement that personal data are processed lawfully. While the Act does not provide any guidance on the meaning of the terms "lawful" or "unlawful", the natural meaning of unlawful has been broadly described by the Courts as "something which is contrary to some law or enactment or is done without lawful justification or excuse". In effect, the Principle means that a data controller must comply with all relevant rules of law whether derived from statute or common law, relating to the purpose and ways in which the data controller processes personal data. The following may be relevant when deciding whether personal data have been processed lawfully:

- Statutory prohibitions on use or disclosure: If the general law prevents a particular disclosure of personal data then there would also be a contravention of the lawful processing requirement of the Data Protection Act 1998 if a disclosure were made.

- The *ultra vires* rule and the rule relating to the excess of delegated powers, under which the data controller may only act within the limits of its legal powers: Public authorities such as the Department of Health or a NHS Trust might exceed their powers if, for instance, they were to make commercial use of patient data, e.g. by selling names and addresses to the manufacturers of medical equipment.

- Contractual restrictions on processing: this may be of particular relevance in the private health sector where the provision of treatment is on the basis of a contract between the patient and the clinician, clinic, hospital etc.

- Confidentiality arising from the relationship of the data controller with the data subject: this issue is considered separately in Chapter 4.

- Article 8 of the European Convention on Human Rights (the right to respect for private and family life, home and correspondence): the Human Rights Act 2000 underpins the Data Protection Act and other legislation. Public authorities are required to construe the legislation under which they operate in accordance with the European Convention on Human Rights and to ensure that their actions and those of their staff are consistent with it.

This list is by no means exhaustive. The various different considerations inevitably overlap. The key issue for the processing of health data is likely to be the common law duty of confidence. This is addressed in greater detail in Chapter 4. In brief, even though the Act does not explicitly require the consent of patients in order to process medical data, in many cases there is an implied requirement to obtain patient consent for the processing of data since to process without consent would involve a breach of a duty of confidence which, in turn, would involve a breach of the requirement in the Act to process personal data lawfully.

Chapter 3: The Second Data Protection Principle

The Second Data Protection Principle states:

> "Personal data shall be obtained only for one or more specified and lawful purposes, and shall not be further processed in any manner incompatible with those purposes."

There are two means by which a data controller may specify the purpose or purposes for which the personal data are obtained:

- In a notice given by the data controller to the data subject in accordance with the fair processing requirements; or

- By notifying the purposes on a data controller's Data Protection Register entry, through the Notification procedures. (It should be noted that Notification to the Commissioner alone will not satisfy the fairness requirements of the First Principle).

These are cumulative and, except in cases where it is proposed to process personal data for purposes that were not envisaged at the time of collection, the information provided to the data subject will reflect the purposes notified to the Commissioner. The effect of the Principle is to reinforce the First Principle and also to limit the range of cases where data may be processed for purposes of which the data subject was not informed to ones which are *compatible* with those for which data were originally obtained.

The Research Exemption

The Act does envisage some exceptions to the Second Principle, notably where personal data are processed for the purposes of research (including statistical or historical purposes). These exceptions are set out in Section 33 of the Act, which is commonly known as 'the research exemption'. These exceptions can be applied where the processing (or further processing) is only for research purposes, and where the following conditions are met:

- The data are not processed to support measures or decisions relating to particular individuals; and

- The data are not processed in such a way that substantial damage or substantial distress is, or is likely to be, caused to any data subject.

Where the exemption applies:

- The further processing of personal data will not be considered incompatible with the purposes for which they were obtained. (It is important to note that the exemption does not excuse the data controller from complying with the part of the Second Principle that states that personal data shall be obtained only for one or more specified and lawful purposes);

- Personal data may be kept indefinitely (despite the Fifth Data Protection Principle which states that personal data should not be kept for longer than is necessary);

- Subject access does not have to be given provided that the results of the research or any resulting statistics are not made available in a form that identifies the data subject.

It is important to note that even where the exemption applies, the data controller is still required to comply with the rest of the Act, including the First and Second Principles. The data controller should ensure that at the time the data are collected, the data subject is made fully aware of what the data controller intends to do with the data. If the data controller subsequently decides to process the data in order to carry out further research of a kind that would not have been envisaged by the data subject at the time the data were collected, the data controller will need to comply with the fair processing requirements of the Act in respect of this processing.

The exemption cannot be used to justify the retention of records for longer than would normally be the case simply because the records might be used for research in the future. The exemption may only be used, in other words, if research is actually being carried out or there is a firm intention to use the records for that purpose.

The research exemption, combined with the special fair processing rules in relation to data obtained from someone other than the data subject, has implications for records based research. Two general cases may be distinguished. In the first case, it is proposed to conduct records based research by making use of current records or ones yet to be created. Patients should be informed, as part of the standard fair processing information, that their data may be used for research purposes designed to better understand and treat their conditions. The research exemption (insofar as compatibility with the Second Principle is concerned) is not relevant since these records will have been compiled both for the purpose of treatment and research.

In the second case, research is proposed using existing records of patients who are no longer being treated for their condition. Such records may be quite old. Those patients who may be contacted without involving disproportionate effort should be given fair processing information. Those patients who cannot be contacted without disproportionate effort need not be given the fair processing information although the researcher should record this fact. The research exemption permits the use of these data for research, providing that the conditions described above apply.

Chapter 4: Confidentiality

Chapter 2 considered, among other matters, the general requirement to process personal data lawfully. While there are potentially a large number of considerations which data controllers processing health data must take, in practice, the key issue in this context is likely to be the duty of confidence.

The duty of confidence is a common law concept rather than a statutory requirement. As such it derives from cases that have been considered by the Courts. Inevitably there are areas which have not been litigated, where it is impossible to state with any certainty whether a duty of confidence exists and, therefore, that the consent of patients is required for the processing of their data. Even where there is case law, it may be difficult to extrapolate general principles from the particular circumstances of the case. There is no certainty that a decision made many years ago by a court would be reflected in a decision made in the context of a modern NHS. In this chapter, we first provide a general introduction to the concept of confidentiality, its exceptions and the requirement to obtain the consent of patients for the processing of medical data. Then we attempt to describe the approach taken by the Commissioner in the area of health.

Confidentiality & Exceptions to the Duty of Confidence

Personal data that are subject to a duty of confidence have a number of characteristics:

* The information is not in the public domain or readily available from another source;

* The information is of a certain degree of sensitivity, (more than "mere tittle tattle") such as medical data;

* The information has been provided with the expectation that it will only be used or disclosed for particular purposes. This expectation may arise because a specific undertaking has been given, because the confider places specific restrictions on the use of data which are agreed by the recipient, or because the relationship between the recipient and the data subject generally gives rise to an expectation of confidentiality, for instance as arises between a customer and a bank or a patient and a doctor.

The Courts have generally recognised three exceptions to the duty of confidence:

* Where there is a legal compulsion;
* Where there is an overriding duty to the public;
* Where the individual to whom the information relates has consented.

Certain disclosures of medical data have long been requirements of the law. Certain diseases are notifiable. More recently s.60 of the Health and Social Care Act 2001 creates a power for the Secretary of State to make orders (subject to various safeguards, and only applicable in England and Wales) requiring the disclosure of patient data that would otherwise be prevented by a duty of confidence. Courts may order the disclosure of patient data in particular cases.

Disclosures required by law are relatively easy to identify. Disclosures that may be justified as being in the public interest, by contrast, necessarily involve the exercise of judgment, balancing the rights of patients against the public good. For instance, a hospital *may* consider the disclosure of medical information to the police would be justified in the event of an assault on a member of staff but unjustified in the context of a minor theft. Because such decisions involve the exercise of judgment it is important that they are taken at an appropriate level and that sound procedures are developed for taking those decisions.

Consent

Most uses or disclosures of medical data will be justified by having obtained the consent of patients. There is no single definition of consent.

The EU Directive, for instance, defines consent as: "*...any freely given specific and informed indication of his wishes by which the data subject signifies his agreement to personal data relating to him being processed.*" On one reading this definition suggests that the giving of consent may not legitimately be made a condition of receiving a service such as health care since to impose conditions might mean that consent had not been "freely given". Were a data controller to seek to rely upon consent as a condition of processing medical data (rather than one of the other possible conditions suggested in Chapter 2) such a strict reading of the definition in the Directive might invalidate the consent that had apparently been obtained.

In considering the common law duty of confidence, however, the courts have not generally found that consent is rendered invalid by having conditions attached, providing that those conditions are not unduly onerous. In considering the common law duty of confidence, it is this approach to consent that the Commissioner will follow, taking three key considerations.

Firstly, consent must be informed. The data subject must know, in other words, what are the proposed uses or disclosures of personal data. In effect a patient will be able to give informed consent if he or she has been supplied with the fair processing information discussed earlier. It follows from this that a patient cannot be deemed to have consented to something of which he or she is ignorant.

Secondly, the person giving consent must have some degree of choice. "Consent" given under duress or coercion is not consent at all. By contrast consent which is entirely optional and may be withheld without any consequences is clearly valid. Between these two extremes is consent which is more or less conditional upon agreement to some other term or condition. It would not necessarily be unfair that a patient should be asked to consent to the disclosure of data by, for example, a GP to a Health Authority for administrative purposes as a condition of receiving treatment from that GP. By contrast it could be argued that a requirement to consent to the disclosure of data to a medical student as a condition of receipt of treatment in a NHS hospital was unfair.

Thirdly, there must be some indication that the data subject has given his or her consent. This may be express (i.e. explicit) or implied. Express consent is given by a patient agreeing actively, usually orally or in writing, to a particular use or disclosure of information. Implied consent is given when an individual takes some other action in the knowledge that in doing so he or she has incidentally agreed to a particular use or disclosure of information. For instance a patient who visits a GP for treatment may be taken to imply consent to the GP consulting his or her medical records to assist diagnosis. The Courts have not generally specified whether consent should be express or implied. It is clear, however, that for consent of any sort to be given, there must be some active communication between the parties. It would not be sufficient, for instance, to write to patients to advise them of a new use of their data and to assume that all who had not objected had consented to that new use. It is a mistake to assume that implied consent is a less valid form of consent than express. Both must be equally informed and both reflect the wishes of the patient. The advantage of express consent is that it is less likely to be ambiguous and may thus be preferred when the risk of misunderstanding is greater.

The Commissioner's approach to medical confidentiality

The Commissioner is not a general source of advice upon confidentiality. However, from time to time, for instance when asked to carry out an assessment of whether the processing of personal data seems likely to meet the requirements of the Act, she must necessarily take a view as to whether firstly, in her opinion, a duty of confidence has arisen and secondly, whether there has been a breach of that duty. Each case must be considered upon its merits. This section of the Guidance describes the general approach.

The Commissioner's general assumption is that the processing of health data (that is data relating to the physical or mental health of data subjects) by a health professional (see Appendix 2) is subject to a duty of confidence even though explicit consent for processing is not a requirement of Schedule 3 of the Act. This assumption is based upon case law, upon statements made by Ministers at the Department of Health, and upon the advice given by regulatory and representative bodies in the area. The Commissioner distinguishes between a number of broad categories.

As was noted earlier, in some cases, even though data may be subject to a duty of confidence, there may be a justification for disclosure or for secondary use. For instance, the disclosure of information relating to a notifiable disease or a disclosure on the basis of an Order made under s.60 of the Health and Social Care Act cannot be legitimately accused of involving breaches of confidence.

Some other uses and disclosures of data, for instance, routine record keeping, consultation of records etc, in the course of the provision of care and treatment or clinical audit are effectively conditions of receiving treatment. Providing that these uses and disclosures are, as a matter of fact, necessary in order to provide treatment in today's National Health Service, the Commissioner thinks that it is unlikely that a court would find that consent was invalid by virtue of being made a condition of treatment. Such uses and disclosures may be described as "mandatory" in the sense that acceptance of treatment by the patient will imply consent to these uses or disclosures. (Although it may be generally acceptable to make the giving of consent a condition of treatment, as is discussed in the next chapter, in individual cases where a particular use or disclosure of personal data might cause unwarranted damage or distress, there is a right to object. For instance consent for administrative staff to access medical data for legitimate administrative purposes might generally be a condition of treatment. However, in a particular case, a patient might object if the member of the administrative team was personally known to him or her.)

In most cases where consent is required in order to satisfy the common law duty of confidence, the Commissioner accepts that implied consent is valid. She does not accept that implied consent is a lesser form of consent. Providing that the fair collection information described in Chapter 2 has been provided at an appropriate time, including information as to whether data must be supplied or whether it is optional to do so, and the data subject accepts treatment and does not object to any uses or disclosures of data, then the Commissioner will consider that valid consent has been given. There is an overlap, in other words, between the fair processing requirements of the Act and the consent requirements of the common law.

The Commissioner does, however, think that there are some occasions when express or explicit consent is required. These arise particularly where data have been collected previously without the relevant fair processing information having been provided. This might occur because data were collected before the Act came into force or because the purposes for which it is proposed that data are processed has changed since collection.

In deciding when express rather than implied consent should be obtained and when it is legitimate to make provision of treatment conditional upon agreement to certain uses or disclosures of personal data, the Commissioner will be influenced not only by any relevant case law but also by any Codes of Practice, advice or guidance issued by the Department of Health, NHS Executive, or any of the relevant representative or regulatory bodies. In individual cases she will also take into account any decision or advice given by Caldicott Guardians, or the Health Service Ombudsman.

Chapter 5: The Right to Object to Processing

The Act does not create an overarching requirement that personal data, even sensitive personal data, may only be processed with the consent of data subjects. As was discussed in Chapter 4, however, in many cases it will only be permissible to process health data with the consent of patients not because this is an explicit requirement of the Data Protection Act but because it is a required by the common law duty of confidence and the Act requires that personal data are processed lawfully.

Although data controllers may not be under a duty to obtain patient consent, there are certainly cases where they should give patients the opportunity to object to the processing of their data. There are also cases where data subjects may legitimately object to the processing of their personal data. These issues are considered in this Chapter.

When should an opt-out be given?

The point was made in Chapter 2 that among the other information that should be provided to data subjects in order to make the processing of personal data fair may be information as to whether the proposed uses or disclosures of data are mandatory or optional. The failure to provide this information would be likely to result in personal data being unfairly collected.

In deciding whether to offer an opt-out, data controllers should attempt to distinguish between those uses and disclosures of data which are essential in order to treat patients within the health service and those which are not. By the term "essential" is meant those uses and disclosures without which treatment could not be given and those uses or disclosures which the law makes mandatory. Examples of essential uses and disclosures include:

- Routine record keeping, consultation of records etc, in the course of the provision of care and treatment;

- Processing of records in the event of a medical emergency;

- Clinical audit e.g. the monitoring of a patient care pathway against existing standards and benchmarks;

- Processing for administrative purposes, e.g. disclosure by a GP made in order to receive payment for treatment provided;

- Administrative audit, which may include studies designed to improve the efficiency of the NHS as an organisation, e.g. to support decisions about the allocation of resources;

- Statutory disclosures to disease registries or statutory disclosures for epidemiological research.

In effect these are necessary elements of the medical purpose for which it is proposed that patients' data are processed. Since it is unlikely to make good administrative sense to offer patients the opportunity to object to the processing of their data for any of the individual elements suggested, it would not make sense to provide an opt-out.

Examples of uses and disclosures that may not be essential include:

- Disclosures to social workers/social services departments;
- Teaching;
- Disclosures to hospital chaplains;
- Clinical trials;
- Disclosures to the media.

In effect these non-essential uses are either for secondary medical purposes, in particular teaching or research, or for non-medical purposes. (Please note: the lists are intended neither to be exhaustive nor to be authoritative. What may be an essential use or disclosure for one data controller may not be essential for another.)

Opt-outs as means of gaining consent

In many cases the requirement of the Data Protection Act to provide fair processing information overlaps with the requirement flowing from the common law duty of confidence to obtain consent for the use and disclosure of data.

For instance, patients register for the first time with, say, a cancer clinic. They are provided with standard fair processing information about uses and disclosures of personal data and are also advised that their records will be made available to researchers who may wish to contact them in the future. Any patients who do not object may be deemed to have consented to the disclosure and to being contacted by the researchers.

It is important to distinguish this case, where patients are registering for the first time and thus have not yet provided the clinic with any personal data, from that where the clinic would like to pass the records of former patients to a researcher. On the assumption that patient consent is required (i.e. there is no relevant order under s.60 of the Health and Social Care Act), and that the research exemption is not relevant (since in this case contact by the researcher might cause substantial distress) it would **not** be sufficient simply to write to former patients giving the opportunity to object. In that case it would be incorrect to infer either consent or an objection from a failure of a patient to respond. The patients would not, in other words, have been given the opportunity to signify consent to the processing of their data.

Where consent to the use or disclosure of personal data is sought after those data were collected, it will normally be necessary to obtain the express or explicit consent of patients.

The Right to Object to Processing

An opt-out should be provided wherever patients have a real choice as to how their data are to be processed or wherever this is an appropriate means of gaining consent. In addition, data subjects also have rights to object to the processing of their data whether or not they have been given an opt-out.

Section 10 of the Act sets out the general right to object:

"... an individual is entitled at any time by notice in writing to a data controller to require the data controller at the end of such period as is reasonable in the circumstance to cease, or not to begin, processing or processing for a specified purpose or in a specified manner, any personal data of which he is the data subject, on the grounds that, for specified reasons –

(a) the processing of those data or their processing for that purpose or in that manner is causing or is likely to cause substantial damage or substantial distress to him or another, and

(b) that damage or distress is or would be unwarranted

Among the important points to note are that objections to processing under this section of the Act must be put in writing, and secondly that the grounds for objection are limited to cases where there is or is likely to be substantial and unwarranted damage or distress to the data subject or another person. (There will be many cases where it is good practice to act upon an objection made by means other than writing. It would also be good practice to respect an individual's wishes even if they could not demonstrate that the damage or distress caused to them was *substantial*.)

A data controller in receipt of a written objection to processing must, within 21 days, inform the person making the objection in writing whether it has complied or intends to comply with the request or must state its grounds for refusing to do so.

The Act gives no comprehensive guidance as to the valid grounds for objecting to the processing of health data, although it makes clear that the interests of the data controller will outweigh those of the person objecting to the processing of data if the processing of data is on the basis of any of the following four Schedule 2 conditions:

•   The data subject has given his consent (this condition will be relevant where the person objecting to the processing is a person other than the data subject);

•   The processing is necessary for the performance of a contract or for entering into a contract at the request of the data subject;

•   The processing is necessary for compliance with legal obligations (for instance a disclosure made on a statutory basis);

•   The processing is necessary to protect the vital interests of the data subject (this condition will also only be relevant where the person objecting to the processing is a person other than the data subject).

In the absence of any clearer guidance in the Act, data controllers must judge each objection to processing which is received on its merits. For instance, two individuals may object to their GP to the processing of their data for administrative purposes. In the case of the first, no grounds for the objection are advanced and the GP may be justified in continuing to process the patient's data for administrative purposes despite the objection (on the assumption that the patient continues to accept treatment). In the second case, a patient objects to the use of data for administrative purposes because a member of the administrative staff in the practice is known to the patient personally and he or she does not wish the details of their medical condition to be disclosed to that person. In this case it is far easier to see that substantial damage or distress might be caused to the patient and it is likely that the GP will decide to make separate administrative arrangements for this patient.

In addition to the general right to object to processing which is, as we have seen, a qualified right, there is an absolute right to object to the use of personal data for direct marketing purposes.

Appendix 1: Practical Application

In this section we seek to apply the analysis of the Principles as discussed in the preceding chapters. Here, the application is limited to those examples listed in the Introduction, but should be sufficiently informative to allow a similar application of the Act to other uses and disclosures of health data.

The tables should not be read in isolation, but in the context of the discussion found in the preceding chapters. Please refer to Chapter 1 for a full description of the use and disclosure headings.

The tables on the following pages are broken down into 4 broad areas:

a)   Care and treatment;
b)   Administration;
c)   Research and teaching;
d)   Uses and disclosures for non-health purposes.

Examples of Uses and Disclosures

a) Care and treatment

Use or Disclosure	Schedule 2 Condition	Schedule 3 Condition	Fair Processing Information	Lawfulness	PETs	2DPP
Routine record-keeping; consultation of records etc	Condition 5 or 6	Condition 8	Ensure patient is aware of identity of data controller. Generally assumed patient is aware of these uses and disclosure.	Consent is likely to be required to meet Common Law obligations but need not be 'explicit' in terms of DPA.	Data must be secure, but there is no general need to use a PET.	Not applicable.
Processing of records in the event of a medical emergency	Condition 5 or 6	Condition 3. Wrong to rely on this condition if patient has previously objected to this type of use.	General information should be provided, even though it could be assumed that patients would expect their data to be available in an emergency.	Consent likely to be required to meet Common Law obligations but need not be 'explicit' in terms of DPA. If patient was unable to consent, then the public interest may meet the Common Law requirements. Common Law would be breached if it was known that the patient objected to the disclosure.	Data must be secure, but there is no general need to use a PET.	Disclosure is compatible.
Disclosures made by one health professional or organisation to another	Condition 5 or 6	Condition 8. Only relevant information should be disclosed.	Any disclosures should be explained.	Consent likely to be required to meet Common Law obligations but need not be 'explicit' in terms of DPA.	Data must be secure, but there is no general need to use a PET.	Disclosure is compatible.

Use or Disclosure	Schedule 2 Condition	Schedule 3 Condition	Fair Processing Information	Lawfulness	PETs	2DPP
Clinical audit	Condition 5 or 6	Condition 8. Only relevant information should be disclosed.	Any disclosures should be explained.	Consent likely to be required to meet Common Law obligations but need not be 'explicit' in terms of DPA.	Strong argument for the use of PETs to protect the identity of patients.	Satisfied by a notice given to patients. Where this was not possible, it may be possible to rely on S33.

b) Administration

Use or Disclosure	Schedule 2 Condition	Schedule 3 Condition	Fair Processing Information	Lawfulness	PETs	2DPP
Processing for administrative purposes	Condition 5 or 6	Condition 8. Only relevant information should be disclosed.	Purposes should be explained in general terms.	Consent likely to be required to meet Common Law obligations but need not be 'explicit' in terms of DPA.	Only disclose patient ID if it is intended to contact the patient. Use of PETs is encouraged.	Disclosure is compatible.
Administrative audit	Condition 5 or 6	Condition 8. Only relevant information should be disclosed.	Uses and disclosures should be explained.	Consent likely to be required to meet Common Law obligations but need not be 'explicit' in terms of DPA.	Strong argument for the use of PETs to protect the identity of patients.	Satisfied by a notice given to patients. If not given, it may be possible to rely on S33.

c) Research and teaching

Use or Disclosure	Schedule 2 Condition	Schedule 3 Condition	Fair Processing Information	Lawfulness	PETs	2DPP
Statutory disclosures to disease registries or statutory disclosures for epidemiological research	Condition 5 or 6	Condition 8. Only relevant information should be disclosed.	Uses and disclosures should be explained.	Common Law obligations met if there is a statutory requirement to disclose e.g. notifiable diseases, or s60 of Health & Social Care Act 2001 (England and Wales only).	Strong argument for the use of PETs to protect the identity of patients.	Satisfied by a notice given to patients. If not given, it may be possible to rely on S33.
Non-statutory disclosures to disease registries or non-statutory disclosures for epidemiological research	Condition 5 or 6	Condition 8. Only relevant information should be disclosed.	Uses and disclosures should be explained, including that this use of personal data is optional.	Consent likely to be required to meet Common Law obligations but need not be 'explicit' in terms of DPA. Patients have the right to object.	Strong argument for the use of PETs to protect the identity of patients.	Satisfied by a notice given to patients. If not given, it may be possible to rely on S33.
Clinical trials	Condition 1, 5 or 6	Condition 1 or 8. Only relevant information should be disclosed.	Uses and disclosures should be explained, including that this use of personal data is optional.	Consent required to meet Common Law obligations and is likely to be 'explicit' in terms of DPA.	Strong argument for the use of PETs to protect the identity of patients.	Satisfied by a notice given to patients. S33 is unlikely to be appropriate.

Use or Disclosure	Schedule 2 Condition	Schedule 3 Condition	Fair Processing Information	Lawfulness	PETs	2DPP
Teaching	Condition 1, 5 or 6	Condition 1 or 8. Only relevant information should be disclosed.	Uses and disclosures should be explained, including that this use of personal data is optional, and whether it is hospital or university based teaching.	Consent likely to be required to meet Common Law obligations, but need not be 'explicit' in terms of DPA. Patients have the right to object.	Strong argument for the use of PETs to protect the identity of patients.	Satisfied by a notice given to patients. S33 is unlikely to be appropriate.

d) Uses and disclosures for non-health purposes

Use or Disclosure	Schedule 2 Condition	Schedule 3 Condition	Fair Processing Information	Lawfulness	PETs	2DPP
Disclosures for Crime and Disorder Act purposes	Condition 5 or 6	Condition 1 or 7. Only relevant information should be disclosed.	Uses and disclosures should be explained, unless prejudicial to S29.	Consent likely to be required to meet Common Law obligations (unless another exception to the duty of confidence applies), but need not be 'explicit' in terms of DPA.	Data must be secure, and anonymised data should be used where possible.	Satisfied by a notice given to patients. If S29 applies, a notice may not be required.
Disclosures to the police	Condition 5 or 6	Condition 7	Uses and disclosures should be explained, unless prejudicial to S29.	Consent not required if disclosure is in the public interest, or if required by law (e.g. court order).	Data must be secure, but there is no general need to use a PET.	Satisfied by a notice given to patients. If S29 applies, a notice may not be required.
Disclosures of religious affiliation to Chaplains	Condition 1. Condition 4 may apply in very limited circumstances.	Condition 1. Condition 3 may apply in very limited circumstances.	Uses and disclosures should be explained.	Consent required, unless individual unable to give consent.	Data must be secure, but there is no general need to use a PET.	Satisfied by obtaining consent of patient.
Disclosures to the media	Condition 1 or 6	Condition 1.	Uses and disclosures should be explained.	Consent likely to be required to meet Common Law obligations.	Data must be secure, but there is no general need to use a PET.	Satisfied by obtaining consent of patient.

Appendix 2: Glossary of Terms

Data controller: A person who (either jointly or in common with other persons) determines the purposes for which and the manner in which personal data are, or are to be, processed.

Data subject: An individual who is the subject of personal data.

Health professional: Means any of the following:

a) a registered medical practitioner (a "registered medical practitioner" includes any person who is provisionally registered under section 15 or 21 of the Medical Act 1983 and is engaged in such employment as is mentioned in subsection (3) of that section.)

b) a registered dentist as defined by section 53(1) of the Dentists Act 1984,

c) a registered optician as defined by section 36(1) of the Opticians Act 1989,

d) a registered pharmaceutical chemist as defined by section 24(1) of the Pharmacy Act 1954 or a registered person as defined by Article 2(2) of the Pharmacy (Northern Ireland) Order 1976,

e) a registered nurse, midwife or health visitor,

f) a registered osteopath as defined by section 41 of the Osteopaths Act 1993,

g) a registered chiropractor as defined by section 43 of the Chiropractors Act 1994,

h) any person who is registered as a member of a profession to which the Professions Supplementary to Medicine Act 1960 for the time being extends,

i) a clinical psychologist, child psychotherapist or speech therapist,

j) a music therapist employed by a health service body, and

k) a scientist employed by such a body as head of department.

Health record: Any record which consists of information relating to the physical or mental health or condition of an individual, and has been made by or on behalf of a

	health professional in connection with the care of that individual.
Personal data:	Data which relate to a living individual who can be identified from those data, or from those data and other information which is in the possession of, or is likely to come into the possession of, the data controller and includes any expression of opinion about the individual and any indication of the intentions of the data controller or any other person in respect of the individual.
Processing:	In relation to information or data, processing means obtaining, recording or holding the information or data, or carrying out any operation or set of operations on the information or data.

Appendix 3: Schedule 2 and Schedule 3 Conditions

Schedule 2:

1. The data subject has given their consent to the processing.

2. The processing is necessary –

   a) for the performance of a contract to which the data subject is a party, or

   b) for the taking of steps at the request of the data subject with a view to entering into a contract.

3. The processing is necessary to comply with any legal obligation to which the data controller is subject, other than an obligation imposed by contract.

4. The processing is necessary in order to protect the vital interests of the data subject.

5. The processing is necessary –

   a) for the administration of justice,

   b) for the exercise of any functions conferred by or under any enactment,

   c) for the exercise of any functions of the Crown, a Minister of the Crown or a government department, or

   d) for the exercise of any other functions of a public nature exercised in the public interest.

6. The processing is necessary for the purposes of legitimate interests pursued by the data controller or by the third party or parties to whom the data are disclosed, except where the processing is unwarranted in any particular case because of prejudice to the rights and freedoms or legitimate interests of the data subject. The Secretary of State may by order specify particular circumstances in which this condition is, or is not, to be taken to be satisfied.

Schedule 3:

1. The data subject has given their explicit consent to the processing of the personal data.

2. The processing is necessary for the purposes of exercising or performing any right or obligation which is conferred or imposed by law on the data controller in connection with employment. The Secretary of State may by order specify cases where this condition is either excluded altogether or only satisfied upon the satisfaction of further conditions.

3. The processing is necessary –

    a) in order to protect the vital interests of the data subject or another person, in a case where-

        i.   consent cannot be given by or on behalf of the data subject, or

        ii. the data controller cannot reasonably be expected to obtain the consent of the data subject, or

    b) in order to protect the vital interests of another person, in a case where consent by or on behalf of the data subject has been unreasonably withheld.

4. The processing –

    a) is carried out in the course of its legitimate activities by any body or association which exists for political, philosophical, religious or trade-union purposes and which is not established or conducted for profit,

    b) is carried out with appropriate safeguards for the rights and freedoms of data subjects,

    c) relates only to individuals who are either members of the body or association or who have regular contact with it in connection with its purposes, and

    d) does not involve disclosure of the personal data to a third party without the consent of the data subject.

5. The information contained in the personal data has been made public as a result of steps deliberately taken by the data subject.

6. The processing –

    a) is necessary for the purpose of, or in connection with, any legal proceedings (including prospective legal proceedings),

    b) is necessary for the purpose of obtaining legal advice, or

    c) is otherwise necessary for the purposes of establishing, exercising or defending legal rights.

7. The processing is necessary –

    a) for the administration of justice,

    b) for the exercise of any functions conferred by or under any enactment, or

    c) for the exercise of any functions of the Crown, a Minister of the Crown or a government department.

The Secretary of State may by order specify cases where this condition is either excluded altogether or only satisfied upon the satisfaction of further conditions.

8. The processing is *necessary* for medical purposes (including the purposes of preventative medicine, medical diagnosis, medical research, the provision of care and treatment and the management of healthcare services) and is undertaken by-

   a) a health professional (as defined in the Act), or

   b) a person who owes a duty of confidentiality which is equivalent to that which would arise if that person were a health professional.

9. The processing –

   a) is of sensitive personal data consisting of information as to racial or ethnic origin,

   b) is necessary for the purpose of identifying or keeping under review the existence or absence of equality of opportunity or treatment between persons of different racial or ethnic origins, with a view to enabling such equality to be promoted or maintained, and

   c) is carried out with appropriate safeguards for the rights and freedoms of data subjects. The Secretary of State may by order specify circumstances in which such processing is, or is not, to be taken to be carried out with appropriate safeguards for the rights and freedoms of data subjects.

10. The personal data are processed in circumstances specified in an order made by the Secretary of State.

Data Protection (Processing of Sensitive Personal Data) Order 2000

Relevant conditions –

7. Processing of medical data or data relating to ethnic origin for monitoring purposes.

9. Processing in the substantial public interest, necessary for the purpose of research whose object is not to support decisions with respect to any particular data subject otherwise than with the explicit consent of the data subject and which is unlikely to cause substantial damage or substantial distress to the data subject or any other person.

INDEX